FROM PARTICLES TO STRINGS TO EXISTENCE: THE THEORY OF EVERYTHING IN MATHEMATICAL LOGIC AND ITS APPLICATIONS TO MEDICAL SCIENCE

THE SEARCH FOR THE THEORY OF EVERYTHING TOOK US TO THE CENTER OF THE UNIVERSE AND GAVE US A GIFT FOR HUMANITY

NISHANTH MEHANATHAN

Made with ♥ on the Notion Press Platform
www.notionpress.com

I dedicate this book to my family, friends, teachers, Lord Krishna, Lord Shani, Goddess Vaishnodevi, and the brothers and sisters of the world. I extend my gratitude to all those who contributed to making this book a reality, which includes everyone I have ever met. Thank you for making this possible and if I offended you please do apologize me. Additionally, I express my gratitude to my friends and teachers who are no longer with us. I believe their strength guided me like angels through challenging times. Thank you, and may you rest in peace.

And lastly I would like to say although I wrote this down, but this solution somehow I feel came from the presence of people I came across, I felt their presence, their manners, their tips and tricks and techniques gave the solution to the problem I was trying to solve as by myself I would hit a wall many a times. So I dedicate this book and its solution as coming from "We the people", Thank you all.

Contents

Contents

Acknowledgements

I would like to express my heartfelt gratitude to my teachers, friends, colleagues, and family members for their unwavering support throughout the process of writing this book. Their guidance and encouragement have been invaluable, and I am forever indebted to them.

The theme of this book has evolved over the past two decades. Exploring the structure of the universe has been a passion of mine since my early days of studying science. I have been driven by the desire to create a comprehensive model that encompasses various fields of knowledge, allowing for a deeper understanding of the universe's intricacies.

I would like to thank the schools of Indian philosophies such as Advaita, Vedanta, Vyakarana, and Samkhya, and philosophers like Bhartrhari, Panini, Yaska, Varsagnya, and many more for inspiring this theory and aiding me in developing a mathematical model based on it.

I would also like to express my gratitude to Shri Krishna, Srila Prabhupada, and ISKCON for guiding me on this journey and allowing me to address this problem. Their presence and blessings have been instrumental in my success.

I would like to thank my company Parabole and our CTO Sandip Bhaumik, who introduced me to the topics of "NLP" and "Digital Twins" which fuelled my quest further.

Lastly, I would like to extend my deepest appreciation to all those who have played a role in shaping this endeavor. Their support and contributions have transformed my vision into a reality, and I am truly grateful for their presence in my life.

Introduction

In this book, we explore the Theory of Everything, drawing from four key fields of formal science: linguistic analysis, set theory, mathematical logic(modal logic) and differential equations. By delving into the science of linguistic analysis, we gain insights into the structure and meaning of language, which serves as a fundamental tool for understanding and communicating knowledge. The set theory provides us with a powerful framework for defining and organizing sets of objects, enabling us to establish relationships and patterns within complex systems. Mathematical logic(modal logic), on the other hand, equips us with the tools to reason and deduce logical conclusions based on rigorous mathematical principles. By integrating these three fields, we aim to uncover the underlying unity and interconnectedness of the Universe, ultimately striving towards a comprehensive and all-encompassing theory that can explain the fundamental nature of our reality.

Pursuing the Theory of Everything involves the application of set theory and mathematical logic(modal logic) to establish a comprehensive framework encompassing all aspects of the Universe. Through the integration of set theory and mathematical logic(modal logic), we strive to unlock the secrets of the Universe and unveil a unified understanding of its intricate workings.

We additionally pursue the proof of the Theory of Everything through linear equations and differential equations.

The technical topics covered include:
The book delves into a range of technical topics that form the foundation of understanding the Universe. These topics include:

1. Exploring the different types of properties or predicates associated with elements of a set of objects.

2. Examining the concept of universal ontology, which seeks to understand the fundamental nature of existence.

3. Investigating the idea of "existence" as an empty entity, exploring its significance and implications.

4. Unraveling the concept of "existence/beingness" as the widest and most pervasive universal attribute.

5. Classifying properties based on their characteristics shedding light on their diverse nature.

6. Exploring a type of string theory and its role in understanding the universe's fundamental structure.

7. Analyzing the applications of these theories and concepts in the field of medical science, uncovering potential insights and advancements.

By studying these technical topics, we aim to deepen our understanding of existence, properties, and their practical applications, providing valuable insights into the nature of our reality and its various domains.

CHAPTER ONE

Universal object ontology through set theory and mathematical logic (modal logic)

Introduction

The pursuit of understanding the theory of everything commences with the formulation of a comprehensive and universally applicable ontology that encompasses all aspects of the Universe. This ontology should be capable of accommodating and accounting for the diverse range of phenomena observed throughout the cosmos. In this context, the Universe is conceptualized as comprising both sentient and insentient objects, as illustrated in Figure 1. These objects collectively form the fundamental constituents of the Universe, serving as the basis for further exploration and analysis. By establishing such a holistic ontology, we strive to develop a framework that captures the essence of the Universe and provides insights into its intricate workings.

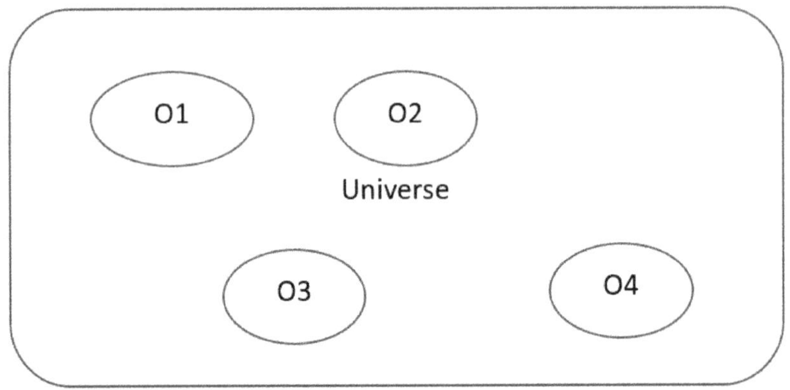

Figure 1. The universe is a collection of sentient and insentient objects

Theorem1:
The types of property or predicate of a set of objects:

1. Universal
2. Differentia
3. Action
4. Imposed property

Proof:
Def. 1: $U = \{O|p\_s(O)\} \cup \{O|p\_ins(O)\}$
Def. 2: $\forall x(O(x) \leftrightarrow (P1(x) \wedge P2(x) \wedge \ldots \wedge PN(x)))$
Ax. 1: $\forall O\ (P(O) \leftrightarrow (Pn(O) \vee Pimp(O)))$.
Ax. 2: $\forall x\ (Pn(x) \leftrightarrow (Pc(x) \vee Pinpc(x)))$.
Ax. 3: $\forall O\ (Pc(O) \leftrightarrow (Ppm(O) \vee Ptmp(O)))$.
Def. 3: $A = S(o1)$ by o.
Ax. 4: $A \leftrightarrow (Inc(A) \vee Dec(A) \vee Change(A) \vee Manifest(A) \vee DeManifest(A) \vee Being(A))$.
Def. 4: $Pinpc \in A$.
Th. 1: $P(x) \leftrightarrow (Ppm(x) \vee Ptmp(x) \vee Pinpc(x) \vee Pimp(x))$.

Explanation:

Def. 1:

U = {O|p_s(O)} ∪ {O|p_ins(O)}

The Universe set is a union of

p_s(O): Object being sentient

p_ins(O): Object being insentient

Def. 2:

For all objects x, O(x) ↔ (P1(x) ∧ P2(x) ∧ ... ∧ PN(x)).

An object is O defined as an entity which has qualifying attributes or property P1, P2, ... PN

Ax. 1:

∀O (P(O) ↔ (Pn(O) ∨ Pimp(O))).

The predicate P represents the properties of an object. The statement asserts that for any object x, its properties P(x) are true if and only if they are either of the natural type Pn(x) or the imposed type Pimp(x). This captures the idea that the properties of an object can be categorized into two possibilities: natural properties or imposed properties.

Ax. 2:

∀x (Pn(x) ↔ (Pc(x) ∨ Pinpc(x))).

The predicate Pn represents the natural properties of an object. The statement asserts that for any object x, its natural properties Pn(x) are true if and only if they are either accomplished Pc(x) or in the process of accomplishment Pinpc(x). This captures the idea that the natural properties of an object can be categorized into two possibilities: accomplished or in the process of accomplishment.

Ax. 3:

∀O (Pc(O) ↔ (Ppm(O) ∨ Ptmp(O))).

Pc is the accomplished natural property of object O

Ppm: The property Pn is permanent

Ptmp: The property Pn is temporary

An inherent property of an object can be of two kinds:

1. Permanent
2. Temporary

The predicate Pc represents the accomplished natural property of an object. The statement asserts that for any object O, Pc(O) is true if and only if it is either Ppm(O) (permanent) or Ptmp(O) (temporary). This captures the idea that the accomplished natural property of an object can be categorized as either permanent or temporary.

Def. 3:

A = S(o1) by o.

A represents the action being performed.

S represents the state change.

o1 represents the object being changed.

o represents the object performing the action.

In this representation, the "=" symbol denotes that the action A is equal to the state change S of object o1 performed by object o.

Ax. 4:

$A \leftrightarrow (Inc(A) \lor Dec(A) \lor Change(A) \lor Manifest(A) \lor DeManifest(A) \lor Being(A))$.

A represents the action being performed. The kinds of actions or becoming that can logically occur are:

Inc(A): "A is an increase."

Dec(A): "A is a decrease."

Change(A): "A is a change."

Manifest(A): "A is manifesting."

DeManifest(A): "A is de-manifesting."

Being(A): represents the statement "A is being."

Therefore, the proposition states that action A is one of the following types: being an increase, decrease, change, manifesting, de-manifesting, or being. These six types of actions/becoming are what an object can become when an action or change over time occurs.

Def. 4:

$Pinpc \in A$.

As shown above Pinpc is such that it belongs to the set of all actions A. property Pinpc is an element of the set of all actions.

The properties or predicate which define a set can be classified as shown in Figure 1.

Th1. :

P(x) ↔ (Ppm(x) ∨ Ptmp(x) ∨ Pinpc(x) ∨ Pimp(x)).

1. Ppm or Generic property, which is permanent and groups into a class.
2. Ptmp or differentia, which is a temporary property and distinguishes an object belonging to a class.
3. Pinpc or action, is a property in the stage of being accomplished.
4. Pimp or an imposed property like a name.

for any object x, the property P(x) is one of the following:
being permanent (Ppm), temporary (Ptmp), in the process of completion (Pinpc), or imposed (Pimp).

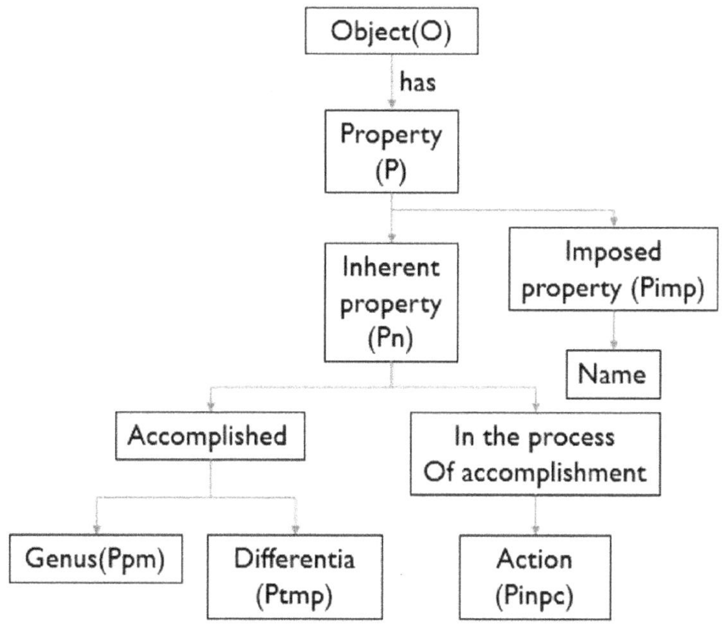

Figure 2. The properties or predicate which define a set

From the above section all properties of an object fall in one of these five categories:

1. Imposed property
2. Generic property
3. Differentia
4. Action
5. Relation (under Differentia category)

These five entities have the properties:

1. They exist (hence occur in an ontology).
2. Are knowable.

And have a name or are denoted by words.

Theroem2:
The universal ontology or types of existence is:
1. Universal
2. Differentia
3. Action
4. Name

Proof:
Def. 1: $E = \{x \mid e(x)\}$
$e(x) \rightarrow \Box(Ex)$
Def. 2: $\exists x\, Ex \rightarrow \Box \exists y\, e(y)$
Ax. 1: $\forall e'\, (Ppm(e') \lor Ptmp(e') \lor Pinpc(e') \lor Pimp(e'))$
Th. 1: $(Ppm \in E \land Ptmp \in E \land Pinpc \in E \land Pimp \in E) \rightarrow (\forall O)(P(O) \leftrightarrow$
$(Ppm(O) \lor Ptmp(O) \lor Pinpc(O) \lor Pimp(O)))$
Def. 3: $Pgns = \{Ppm \mid (\forall Ppm)(C1(Ppm))\}$
Def. 4: $Pdff = \{Ptmp \mid (\forall Ptmp)(C2(Ptmp))\}$
Def. 5: $Pactn = \{Pinpc \mid (\forall Pinpc)(C3(Pinpc))\}$
Def. 6: $Pnm = \{Pimp \mid (\forall Pimp)(C4(Pimp))\}$

Explanation:
Def. 1:
$E = \{x \mid e(x)\}$
$e(x) \rightarrow \Box(Ex)$

In this representation, E represents the "Existence" set, and e(x) represents the property of x having existence. The notation □(Ex) represents the modal operator "necessity" indicating that the proposition Ex (x exists) is necessary or always true. The arrow (→) represents implication, stating that if x has the property of existence (e(x)), then it is necessary that x exists (□(Ex)).

Def. 2:

$\exists x\ Ex \rightarrow \Box \exists y\ e(y)$

If there exists an object x that has existence, then it is necessary that there exists an object y that has the property of existence.

Ax. 1:

$\forall e'\ (Ppm(e') \vee Ptmp(e') \vee Pinpc(e') \vee Pimp(e'))$

For all e', it is true that e' exists in Permanent property (Ppm) or in differentia (Ptmp), or in action (Pinpc), or in imposed property (Pimp).

Th. 1:

$(Ppm \in E \wedge Ptmp \in E \wedge Pinpc \in E \wedge Pimp \in E) \rightarrow (\forall O)(P(O) \leftrightarrow (Ppm(O) \vee Ptmp(O) \vee Pinpc(O) \vee Pimp(O)))$

If Ppm belongs to the "Existence" set, Ptmp belongs to the "Existence" set, Pinpc belongs to the "Existence" set, and Pimp belongs to the "Existence" set, then for all objects O, the property P(O) is equivalent to Ppm(O) or Ptmp(O) or Pinpc(O) or Pimp(O).

Def. 3,4,5 and 6:

$Pgns = \{Ppm \mid (\forall Ppm)(C1(Ppm))\}$

$Pdff = \{Ptmp \mid (\forall Ptmp)(C2(Ptmp))\}$

$Pactn = \{Pinpc \mid (\forall Pinpc)(C3(Pinpc))\}$

$Pnm = \{Pimp \mid (\forall Pimp)(C4(Pimp))\}$

C1(Ppm): Genus properties are permanent and static and the basis for the name of an object.

C2(Ptmp_nch): Differentia serves to distinguish objects within the same class and can change or are temporary.

C3(Ptmp_ch): Actions are properties in the state of accomplishment and have stages or activities which follow in a series.

C4(Pimp): Imposed properties are artificial and imposed by will like a name.

Pgns = set of genus properties
Pdff = set of differentia
Pactn = set of actions
Pnm = set of imposed properties

Figure 3 shows a sample set of generic properties, actions, differentia and imposed properties

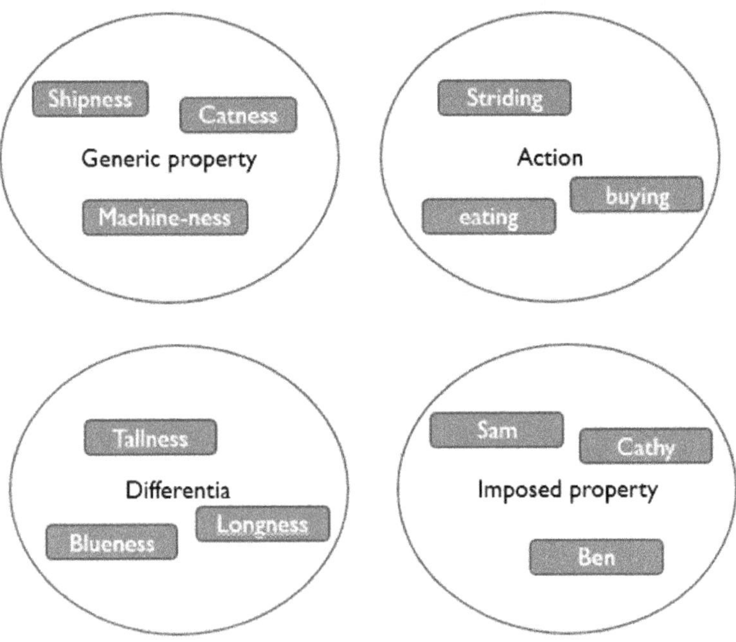

Figure 3. The set of generic property, action, differentia and imposed property

Figure 4 shows the entities possessing "Existence". Which is all the types of predicates/properties of a set. So the property of "existing/being" is a unifying characteristic hence it is a generic characteristic or class found in all of the entities shown in Figure 4.

So we observe that all these objects are a manifestation of "Existence" or a type of the class "Existing".

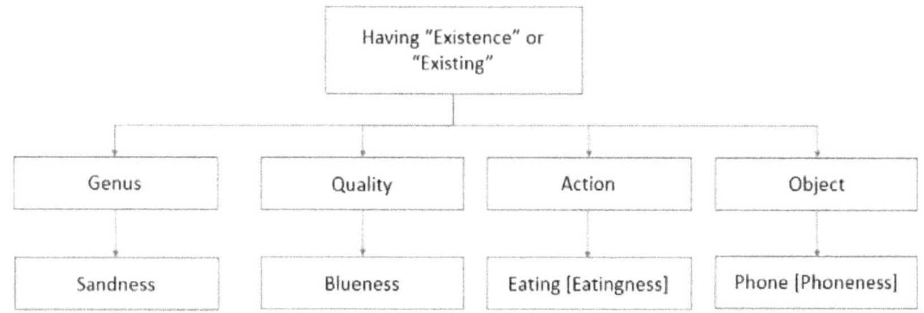

Figure 4. Category of "Existing/Being" or objects having "Existence/Beingness."

And "Existence" is one as "Existence" in Object A isn't different from "Existence" in Object B their nature is the same. They (Existence) have no special distinguishing mark, so they are one.

We can see from the above tree that "Existing" is the highest genus as "Existence/Beingness" is found in everything (Objects, Quality and Action). The different Universals are nothing, but "Existence/Beingness" as they occur in a particular object/entity. So Cow-ness is nothing but "Existence/Beingness" as it exists in a cow and Hero-ness is nothing but "Existence/Beingness" as it exists in a hero this is shown in Figure 5.

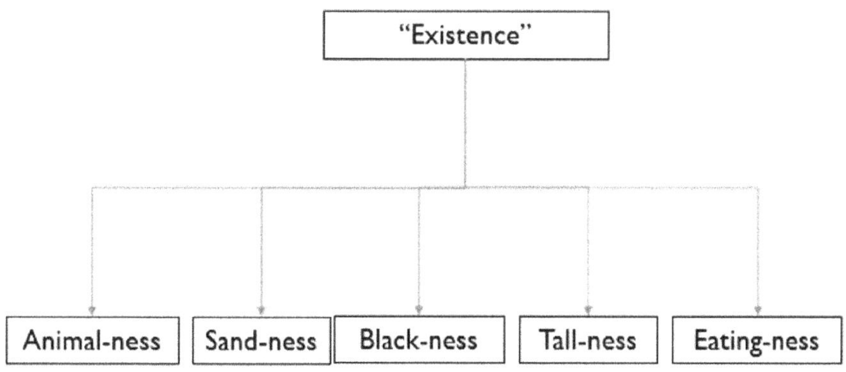

Figure 5. "Existence" is the highest genus, the genus tree

Everything falls in the class of "Existence" so it is the highest genus, everything is a manifestation of existence. Everything is hence a type of existence.

CHAPTER TWO

Understanding Existence to understand the Universe and Theorems on it

Generic property/class "Existence":
"Existence" is the "state of Existing". Generic property/class "Existence" is an entity, as we had discussed earlier that generic property is one of the five entities that exist.

Treating this generic property as an object and this object has the property that it is "Existing" or "it is" and has no other property, so it is an "empty entity" or as it is existing (in a self-existent fashion). So everything is a type of "existent/existing" or "Existence".

P(Existence): exists
Everything that exists has this property hence everything is a type of Existence, or falls in this category.

Everything $\in$ E
E: The set of existence
E = $\{x|P(x)\}$
P(x) = x exists

Theorem 3:
Existence is an empty entity.

Proof:

Def. 1: $E = \{\, x \mid e(x)\}$

Def. 2: $e(x) =$ It exists

Def. 3: e': $e' \in E$

Def. 4: $\neg \exists P(e')$

Th. 1: $P(e') = \{\}$

Explanation:

Def. 1 and Def. 2:

The existent class is E as shown in Def 1, the predicate is that x exists.

Def. 3:

e' or "Existence" belongs to this class as it is self-existent, All we can say about "Existence" is that "it is".

Def. 4:

$\neg$ symbol denotes negation, $\exists$ symbol represents existential quantification, and $P(e')$ represents the property P applied to the entity e'. The proposition $\neg\exists P(e')$ states that there does not exist any property P that applies to the entity e'. This indicates the absence of properties for the existence of e', implying that e' does not possess any properties. Other than the fact that it exists.

Th. 1:

The properties of Existence are an empty set as shown in equation Th 1.

Theorem 4:

"Existence/Beingness" is the widest persistence universal:

Proof:

Def. 1: $P1(O1) \wedge P3(O1) \wedge E(O1) \wedge (O1, Pt1)$.

Def. 2: $P1(O1') \wedge P4(O1') \wedge E(O1') \wedge (O1', Pt2)$.

Def. 3: $P1(O1'') \wedge P5(O1'') \wedge E(O1'') \wedge (O1'', Pt3)$

Def. 4: $P1(O) \wedge P1(O1)$.

Ax. 1: $\forall m \in M(O), e' \to m$.

Th. 1: $Pw(e')$.

Explanation:

Def. 1:

$P1(O1) \wedge P3(O1) \wedge E(O1) \wedge (O1, Pt1)$

Let O1 represent the object.
Let P1 represent the property.
Let P3 represent another property.
Let Pt1 represent a specific time.
Let E(O1) represent the statement "O1 exists."
Therefore, the proposition states that object O1 has property P1, property P3, and existence E(O1) at time Pt1.

Def. 2:

$P1(O1') \wedge P4(O1') \wedge E(O1') \wedge (O1', Pt2)$

Let O1' represent the changed object O1.
Let P1 represent a property.
Let P4 represent another property.
Let Pt2 represent a specific time.
Let E(O1') represent the statement "O1' exists."
Therefore, the proposition states that the changed object O1', which was derived from O1, has property P1, property P4, and existence E(O1') at time Pt2.

Def. 3:

$P1(O1'') \wedge P5(O1'') \wedge E(O1'') \wedge (O1'', Pt3)$

Let O1'' represent the changed object O1'.
Let P1 represent a property.
Let P5 represent another property.
Let Pt3 represent a specific time.
Let E(O1'') represent the statement "O1'' exists."
Therefore, the proposition states that the changed object O1'', which was derived from O1', has property P1, property P5, and existence E(O1'') at time Pt3.

Def. 4:

$P1(O) \wedge P1(O1).$

Let P1 represent the property.
Let O represent the object.
Let O1 represent the modified object.
Therefore, the proposition states that the property P1 holds true for both the object O and the modified object O1.]

Ax. 1:

$\forall m \in M(O), e' \to m.$

Let e' represent the generic property existence. Let O represents the object.

Let M(O) represents the set of all modifications of object O.

The proposition states that for every modification m in the set of all modifications M(O) of object O, the generic property existence e' follows.

Generic property existence e' follows all modifications of Object O

Th. 1:

Pw(e')

This proposition states that the generic property existence e' has the property Pw of having the widest persistence.

Generic property existence e' has the property Pw of having the widest persistence

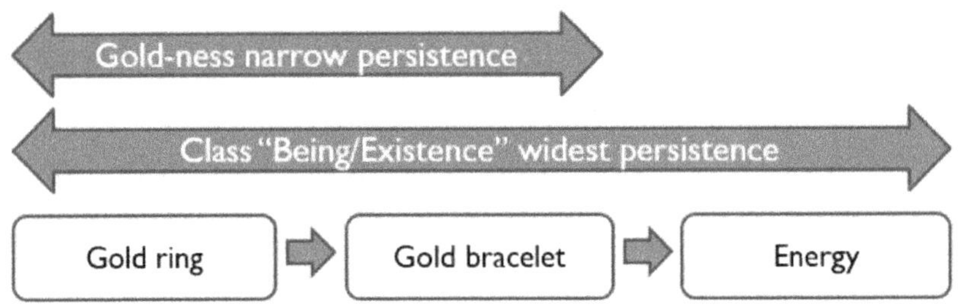

Figure 1. Class "Existence" has the widest persistence

We see that the Universal "Existence" has the widest persistence as seen in Figure 1. So the generic quality "Being/Existing" or "Existence" is an inseparable quality.

Object and Name

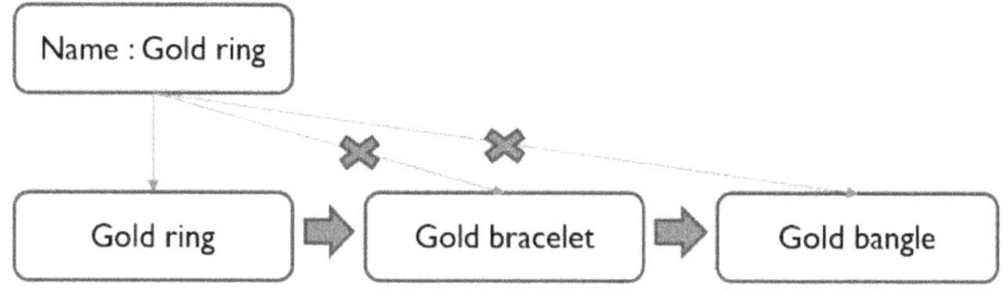

Figure 2. The Name and object relation is not permanent

The relation between the word and the denoted object must be permanent, if it is not so then the word would not refer to the object it was referring to initially an example is shown in Figure 2. The word must be based on something in the object which is permanent such that the relation between the word and the denoted object is permanent.

Theorem 5:
Existence is everywhere and in everything:

Proof:
Def. 1: $E = \{x \mid e(x)\}$
Def. 2: $p(O)$
Ax. 1: $Ppm(p) \lor Ptmp(p) \lor Pinpc(p) \lor Pimp(p)$.
Ax. 2: $\forall x, (U(x) \lor D(x) \lor A(x) \lor I(x)) \rightarrow E(x)$.
Ax. 3: $\forall x ((S(x) \lor I(x)) \rightarrow E(x))$
Th. 1: $\forall x (U(x) \rightarrow E(x))$

Explanation:
Def. 1:
$E = \{x \mid e(x)\}$
The "Existence set" has element x such that x has "Existence" or x "Exists".

Def. 2:
$p(O)$
O is such that O has property P

Ax. 1:

Ppm(p) ∨ Ptmp(p) ∨ Pinpc(p) ∨ Pimp(p)

Let Ppm(p) represent the statement "p is a permanent property."

Let Ptmp(p) represent the statement "p is a temporary property."

Let Pinpc(p) represent the statement "p is in the process of completion."Let Pimp(p) represent the statement "p is an imposed property."

Property p is such that p is Ppm(Universal), Ptmp(Differentia), Pinpc(Action), Pimp(Imposed property)

Ax. 2:

∀x, (U(x) ∨ D(x) ∨ A(x) ∨ I(x)) → E(x)

Let E(x) represent the statement "x exists."

Let U(x) represent the statement "x has the property of being Universal."

Let D(x) represent the statement "x has the property of being Differentia."

Let A(x) represent the statement "x has the property of being an Action."

Let I(x) represent the statement "x has the property of being an Imposed property."

The proposition states that for all objects x, if x has the property of being Universal, Differentia, an Action,

or an Imposed property, then x exists.

This proposition asserts that the existence of "Existence" pervades all objects and properties, thereby indicating that they exist.

All the properties like Universal, differentia, action and imposed property have existence, So all objects and properties are pervaded by "Existence" hence they exist

Ax. 3:

∀x ((S(x) ∨ I(x)) → E(x))

S(x): Predicate representing "x is a sentient object."

I(x): Predicate representing "x is an insentient object."

E(x): Predicate representing "x exists."

U(x): Predicate representing "x belongs to the universe U."

The first equation states that for every object x, if x is either a sentient or an insentient object, then x exists. This captures the idea that all objects within the universe, whether sentient or insentient, have existence.

Th. 1:

∀x (U(x) → E(x))

S(x): Predicate representing "x is a sentient object."

I(x): Predicate representing "x is an insentient object."
E(x): Predicate representing "x exists."
U(x): Predicate representing "x belongs to the universe U."
The second equation states that for every object x in the universe U, x exists. This represents the idea that existence pervades all objects in the universe U.

Theorem 6:
Existence is everything:

Proof:
Def. 1: $E = \{x \mid e(x)\}$
Ax. 1: $(U(x) \land E(x)) \rightarrow \forall y, E(y)$.
Th. 1: $\{x \mid x \in E, e''(x)\}$

Explanation:
Def. 1:
$E = \{x \mid e(x)\}$
The "Existence set" has element x such that x has universal "Existence" or x "Exists".

Ax. 1:
$(U(x) \land E(x)) \rightarrow \forall y, E(y)$
Let U(x) represents the statement "x belongs to the Universe set." Let E(x) represents the statement "x belongs to the Existence set."
x is such that x belongs to the Universe set and x belongs to the "Existence" set,
this implies that everything exists.
The proposition states that if x belongs to both the Universe set and the Existence set, then it implies that for all y, y belongs to the Existence set.
This proposition asserts that if something belongs to the Universe set and the Existence set, then it implies that everything exists, as denoted by the statement $\forall y, E(y)$.

Th. 1:
$\{x \mid x \in E, e''(x)\}$
x is such that x belongs to the "Existence" set, and x is a type of "Existence" or "Existence" as it manifests. "Existence" never manifests as itself, but in

instances which have other properties as well.

This is the unification theory in short that everything is a manifestation of or instance of "Existence". In the next section we look at the attributes of "Existence".

"Existence/Being" is manifested as everything mobile and immobile in the universe.

Everything is an "Existence" or a type of it, this is because Existence is distinguished by the fact that "it exists" and all other things too have this quality that "they exist" hence they are also "Existence" and a type of it.

1. It is defined and undefined.
2. It is manifest and unmanifest.
3. The housed and houseless.
4. Whatever exists it is.
5. Supports the cosmic manifestation.
6. Cause of all activities.
7. The material cause of the Universe.
8. It is outside and inside.
9. It is non-moving and moving.
10. It is far and near.
11. The supporter, destroyer, creator of all beings and controller of the Universe.
12. Indestructible.
13. Formless and with form.
14. Everything and everywhere.
15. Sees through all eyes, hears through all ears, eats through all mouths, feels through all hearts, thinks through all minds, and reasons through all intellects, as he is everything.
16. Has innumerable hands and legs.
17. With hands and feet everywhere, with eyes, heads, and mouths everywhere, with ears everywhere, he encompasses everything in the world.
18. Existence is fire, sun, air, stars, and the moon.
19. It is woman, it is man, it is the youth. it is the maiden too. It is the old man who totters along, leaning on the staff.
20. It is the thundercloud, the seasons, and the oceans. It is without a beginning. It is the Infinite. It is from whom all the worlds are born.

21. It possesses countless heads. All heads, all eyes, all hands, and all feet belong to "Existence". It works through all hands, eats through all mouths, sees through all eyes, hears through all ears, walks through all feet, and thinks through all minds.

22. It is the internal ruler of the universe.

23. It is great because, as the sun it gives heat and light, as the moon it gives light, as earth food and shelter, as the oceans and rivers water as your father, mother, brother and sister love and affection.

24. The enjoyer, the enjoyed and the enjoyment.

25. Appearing as Many due to the multiplicity of its powers.

26. It is the creator, destroyer, and preserver of everything.

CHAPTER THREE

Classification of qualities

An accomplished or static quality is of two types:

1. Generic Quality: Attributes that persistently exist within an object throughout its lifespan are referred to as "generic qualities." These qualities possess a unique characteristic of unifying objects into a genus or class based on their presence in individuals. This concept of generic qualities highlights their role in categorizing and classifying objects based on their shared attributes.
2. Differentia: Attributes which distinguish objects within a class, change over time and are not found permanently with the object are called "Qualities" or "Differentia".

These qualities have been discussed in chapter 1.

Classification of properties:
These static qualities can be further classified as:

1. Perceptible (Has an effect on the senses or are objects of the senses).
2. Imperceptible (Cannot be perceived)

The perceptible property is experienced by its action on the senses and the imperceptible property is inferred from its perceptible effect/action on an object.

Theorem 7:
The properties of an object are good, bad and partly good and bad

Proof:

Def. 1: O:P(O)

Ax. 1: Imp(P) ∨ Per(P)

Ax. 2: Per(P) ⇒ S(A)

Ax. 3: Imp(P) ⇒ P(A)

Ax. 4: (P → S(A) ∨ P → O(A)) ∧ E(P).

Ax. 5: A ⇒ R

Ax. 6: Pg(R) ∨ Pb(R)

Ax. 7: Pg(R) ⇒ Pl

Ax. 8: Pb(R) ⇒ Pn

Th. 1: P' = Pg' ∪ Pb'.

Explanation:

Def. 1:

O:P(O)

Object O is such that O has property P.

Ax. 1:

Imp(P) ∨ Per(P)

Let P represent the property.

Let Imp(P) represent the statement "P is imperceptible."

Let Per(P) represent the statement "P is perceptible."

Property P is such that P is Imp(imperceptible) or Per(perceptible).

Ax. 2:

Per(P) ⇒ S(A)

The perceptible property produces actions on the senses S(A)

Ax. 3:

Imp(P) ⇒ P(A)

Imperceptible properties cause perceptible actions P(A)

Ax. 4:

(P → S(A) ∨ P → O(A)) ∧ E(P)

Let P represent the property.

Let S(A) represent the statement "Action A affects the senses."

Let O(A) represent the statement "Action A affects objects."

Let E(P) represent the statement "Property P has existence.
Property P has the attribute that it produces action on senses or perceptible action on an object and it has "Existence".

Ax. 5:

$A \Rightarrow R$

Any action A produces result R

Ax. 6:

$Pg(R) \vee Pb(R)$

Let R represents the result.
Let Pg(R) represent the statement "Result R has the property of being good."
Let Pb(R) represents the statement "Result R has the property of being bad."
Therefore, the proposition states that the result R either has the property of being good (Pg(R)) or the property of being bad (Pb(R)).
Result R has the property Pg(being good) or Pb(being bad)

Ax. 7:

$Pg(R) \Rightarrow Pl$

Pg(R) Good results produce pleasure

Ax. 8:

$Pb(R) \Rightarrow Pn$

Pb(R) bad results produce pain

Th. 1:

$P' = Pg' \cup Pb'$

Let P' represent the set of all properties.
Let Pg' represent the set of good properties.
Let Pb' represent the set of bad properties.

Therefore, the proposition states that the set of all properties, P', is equal to the union of the set of good properties, Pg', and the set of bad properties, Pb'. This implies that P' contains properties that fall into these different categories.
So Any property experienced falls under the category of good, bad, or both good and bad as shown in Figure 1.

Here good is defined as what is pleasant or agreeable and gives pleasure and bad is defined as what is unpleasant and disagreeable and gives pain. Hence the properties of an object can also be classified into three categories:

1. Only good property and having no badness.
2. Only bad property and having no goodness.
3. Partly Good and partly bad or a mixed property i.e. it is partly good and partly bad.

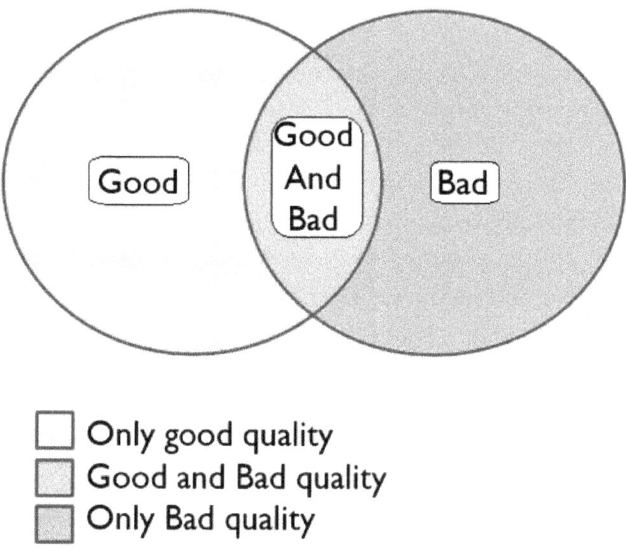

Figure 1. Classification of Qualities based on experience

This is the way qualities(properties) are classified, examples will be given for the three qualities and an explanation of how it works, bad opposes good and good opposes bad and good gives pleasure and bad gives pain.

1. An example of good physical quality is strength, spring constant etc, as stronger something is the better. In terms of mental qualities examples of good qualities are kindness, affection, non-violence, gratitude etc.
2. An example of partly good quality(physical) is Force it causes motion or acceleration which is its good aspect and it causes deformation and

bending etc. which is its bad aspect as deformation and bending can lead to destruction of the object. In terms of mental qualities the list includes courage, rumination, determination etc.

3. An example of bad quality(physical) is mass M and resistance R which cause inertia in their respective actions of acceleration and current flow. The slowing down of action is a bad trait. Bad mental qualities include laziness, disgust, attachment, depression, helplessness etc.

An example set is [spring constant, K; Force, F; Mass m], here good aspect of force F causes acceleration and the bad quality mass m opposes this good aspect to deaccelerate the mass.

The bad aspect of Force F is that it deforms the object and this is opposed by the good quality spring constant K.

Now we know that goodness(giving pleasure or agreeable) and badness(painful or disagreeable), are opposite of each other in nature and effect, mathematically speaking good is the reciprocal of it, as it has a nature which is opposite of it. So goodness is agreeable and badness disagreeable. From the graph for badness as shown in Figure 2, we can see that absence of bad quality is agreeable or negation of bad quality is an attribution of good quality which is opposite in nature. We can conclude that absence of bad quality is presence of the opposite good quality or negation of bad quality is the attribution of the opposite good quality.

From the graph for good Figure 3, we see this doesn't hold the other way round, that is the negation of good quality doesn't imply the attribution of bad qualities

Figure 2. Graph for Badness vs Disagreeability

Figure 3. Graph for Goodness vs Agreeability

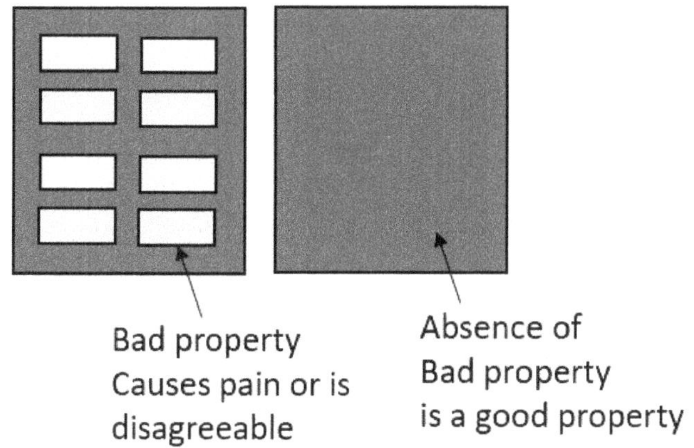

Figure 4. Absence of Bad property is a good property

Theorem 8:

Good property is the absence of bad property, or good property is the opposite of bad property

Proof:

Def. 1: P'(O)

Ax. 1: P = Pg ∪ Pb

Def. 2: P' $\in$ P

Ax. 2: Pb' $\rightarrow$ (Ab $\rightarrow$ (R $\wedge$ Da(R))).

Ax. 3: $\exists$x (Ex $\wedge$ Bx)

Ax. 4: $\neg$P $\square$ Q

Ax. 5: $\neg\Diamond$Pb' $\leftrightarrow$ $\square\neg$Pb' v $\Diamond$Pg

Th. 1: Pg' $\leftrightarrow$ $\neg$Pb'

Explanation:

Def. 1:

P'(O)

Object O is such that O has property P'

Ax. 1 and Def. 2:

P = Pg $\cup$ Pb

P' $\in$ P

The Set of all properties P is the union of the set of all good properties Pg
and the set of all bad properties Pb

Property P' belongs to set P

Ax. 2:

Pb' $\rightarrow$ (Ab $\rightarrow$ (R $\wedge$ Da(R))).

Let Pb' represent the set of bad properties. Let Ab represent the action
associated with the bad property.

Let R represent the result.

Let Da(R) represent the statement "Result R has the property of being
undesirable."

Bad property Pb' produces bad action Ab which produces bad result R such
that R has property Da of being undesirable.

Ax. 3:

$\exists$x (Ex $\wedge$ Bx),

where:

$\exists$x denotes the existential quantifier, indicating that there exists an object x
satisfying the following conditions.

Ex represents the existence of object x.

Bx denotes the property x is the bad property Pb'

Ax. 4:

¬P □ Q

"presence of bad property Pb'" as P and the property "absence of bad property Pb'" as Q

It is not the case that bad property Pb' is present, and it is necessary that bad property Pb' is absent.

Ax. 5:

¬◇Pb' ↔ □¬Pb' v ◇Pg

   ¬ is the negation symbol (not).

◇ represents the possibility operator (sometimes read as "eventually" or "possibly").

□ represents the necessity operator (sometimes read as "always" or "necessarily").

Pb' represents the bad property.

Pg represents the good property.

   The statement can be read as follows: "The opposite of the possibility of having the bad property Pb' is equivalent to the necessity of not having the bad property Pb' or the possibility of having the good property Pg."

Th. 1:

Pg' ↔ ¬Pb'

From the above steps we can conclude that good property Pg' is the absence of bad property Pb' as shown in Figure 4.

   In terms of mathematical equations

   G = Good property

   B = Bad property

   G = 1 / B

Theorem 9:

Negation or absence of good property is not bad property but extraordinary good property

Proof:

Def. 1: P'(O)

Ax. 1: P = Pg ∪ Pb

Def. 2: P' ∈ P

Ax. 2: Pg' $\rightarrow$ (Ag $\rightarrow$ (R $\land$ Agr(R))).

Ax. 3: $\exists$x (Ex $\land$ Gx)

Ax. 4: $\neg$P $\square$ Q

Ax. 5: $\neg\lozenge$Pg' $\leftrightarrow$ $\square\neg$Pg' $\leftrightarrow$ $\square\neg$Pb' $\leftrightarrow$ v $\lozenge$Peg'

Th. 1: Peg' $\leftrightarrow$ $\neg$Pg'

Explanation:

Def. 1:

P'(O)

Object O is such that O has property P'

Ax. 1 and Def. 2:

P = Pg $\cup$ Pb

P' $\in$ P

The Set of all properties P is the union of the set of all good properties Pg
and the set of all bad properties Pb

Property P' belongs to set P

Ax. 2:

Pg' $\rightarrow$ (Ag $\rightarrow$ (R $\land$ Agr(R))).

Let Pg' represent the set of good properties. Let Ag represent the action
associated with the good property.

Let R represent the result.

Let Agr(R) represent the statement "Result R has the property of being
agreeable."

Good property Pg' produces good action Ag which produces good result R
such that R has property Agr of being agreeable.

Ax. 3:

$\exists$x (Ex $\land$ Gx),

where:

$\exists$x denotes the existential quantifier, indicating that there exists an object x
satisfying the following conditions.

Ex represents the existence of object x.

Gx denotes the property x is the good property Pg'

Ax. 4:

¬P □ Q

"presence of good property Pg'" as P and the property "absence of good property Pg'" as Q

Opposite of presence of good property Pg' is absence of Pg'.

Ax. 5:

¬◇Pg' ↔ □¬Pg' ↔ □¬Pb' v ◇Peg'

   ¬ is the negation symbol (not).

◇ represents the possibility operator (sometimes read as "eventually" or "possibly").

□ represents the necessity operator (sometimes read as "always" or "necessarily").

Pb' represents the bad property.

Pg represents the good property.

   The statement can be read as follows: "The opposite of the possibility of having the good property Pg' is equivalent to the necessity of not having the good property Pg' or of not having the bad property Pb' or the possibility of having the extraordinary good property Peg'."

Th. 1:

Peg' ↔ ¬Pg'

From the above steps we can conclude that the extraordinarily good property Peg' is the absence of good property Pg' as shown in Figure 5.

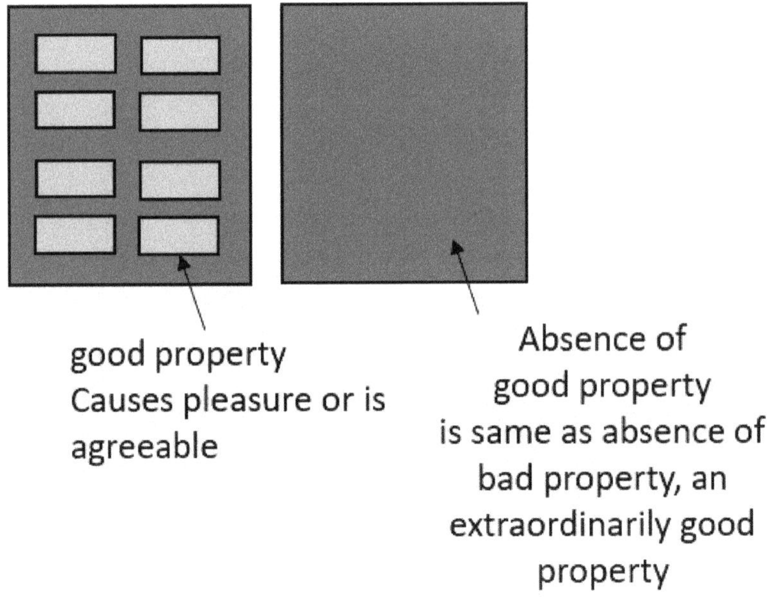

Figure 5. Absence of normal good property is same as the absence of a
bad property or presence of an extraordinarily good property

Theorem 10:

Badness is the existing entity, goodness is its absence and opposite

Proof:

Lets assume that good exists and for example we take sugar and mix it in water the water is sweet now in the situation that there is no sugar or goodness in water it is not bad or bitter and not bad or not bitter is not pain or pleasure so absence of goodness is not pain or is pleasure or still good, as good is not opposite of bad good is not an existential quality.

Let's define the following propositions:

G: Goodness exists.

S: Sugar is present.

W: Water is sweet.

B: Water is bad.

R: Water is bitter.

P: Water is pleasurable.

A: Absence of goodness.

Representing the statements in logical equations:

a. "Good exists and when sugar is mixed in water, the water is sweet."

$G \land (S \to W)$

b. "In the situation where there is no sugar or goodness in water, it is not bad or bitter."

$(\neg S \lor \neg G) \to (\neg B \lor \neg R)$

c. "Not bad or not bitter is not pain or pleasure."

$\neg B \lor \neg R \to P$

d. "The absence of goodness is not pain or is pleasure or still good."

$A \to \neg Pain \to P \lor G$

e. "Good is not the opposite of bad; hence good is not an existential quality."

$\neg(G \leftrightarrow B)$

$\neg \exists x\, G$

Lets assume bad exists and its opposite is good or absence of bad. It is agreeable so is not pain or is pleasure or good which is true. As an analogy, if we add bromine in water it is bad or disagreeable its absence is agreeable or not pain and is pleasure which is good, so the opposite of bad is good and good is the opposite of bad and good is the absence of bad. So we notice that the opposition holds only when badness is the existing entity and goodness an absence of it.

To represent the logical relationships described in the paragraph, we can break down the statements and express them using logical equations. Here's a step-by-step breakdown:

1. Let's define the following propositions:

- B: Badness exists.

- G: Goodness exists.

- A: Absence of badness.

- R: It is agreeable.

- P: It is pain.

- Q: It is pleasure.

- G': Good

2. Representing the statements in logical equations:

a. "Bad exists and its opposite is good or absence of bad":

$B \land (\neg B \leftrightarrow (G \lor A))$

b. "It is agreeable so it is not pain or is pleasure or good":

$R \to (\neg P \lor Q \lor G)$

c. "If we add bromine in water, it is bad or disagreeable. Its absence is agreeable or not pain and is pleasure which is good":

$(\text{Bromine} \to B) \land (\neg \text{Bromine} \to R) \land (\neg \text{Bromine} \to (R \lor \neg P \lor Q \lor G'))$

d. "The opposite of bad is good and good is the opposite of bad and good is the absence of bad":

$(\neg B \leftrightarrow G) \land (G \leftrightarrow \neg B) \land (G \leftrightarrow A)$

CHAPTER FOUR

The qualities of Existence

Existence is the fundamental state of being, the state of actually existing or being present in reality. It encompasses the notion of being and is the basis for all existence in the universe. It signifies the presence and reality of an entity or object, indicating its tangible or intangible existence. The concept of existence extends beyond physical objects and includes abstract entities, ideas, and even the existence of relationships and phenomena. Understanding the nature and essence of existence is a fundamental inquiry that has captivated philosophers, scientists, and thinkers throughout history.

The attribute of existence is inherently tied to its own existence, as it signifies the state of being present or real. It is a self-referential quality, as its essence lies in its own existence. Existence is not merely a concept or idea, but a fundamental aspect of reality that encompasses all things that exist. It is the foundation upon which everything else in the universe relies, forming the basis for all experiences, perceptions, and interactions. Recognizing the attribute of existence brings forth an appreciation for the profound nature of being and the interconnectedness of all existence.

The attribute of Existence is Q1: [it exists]

it has no other attributes, in terms of the three types of properties all three of them are 0: So the quality of existence is:

$Qe = Q1 + 0(\text{only good}) + 0(\text{only bad}) + 0(\text{good and bad})$
$Qe = [\text{It exists}] + \text{absence of all good qualities} + \text{absence of all bad qualities}$

From the above section absence of all bad qualities is equivalent to the presence of all good qualities.

And as a good quality is opposite in nature to a bad quality it is inversely proportional, this implies that 0 of a negative quality corresponds to infinity of the opposite positive quality as shown in Figure 1.

Theorem 11:
Existence is the collection of all good qualities and it is sentient

Proof:
Def. 1: $O|P'(O)$
Ax. 1: $P = Pg \cup Pb$
Def. 2: $P' \in P$
Ax. 2: $Pg'(O) = \sim Pb'(O)$
Def. 3: $e' \in E$,
Ax. 3: $P\_ e' = \{\}$
Ax. 4: $\neg Pb' \Rightarrow Pg'$
Ax. 5: $P\_ e' = \{\neg Pb1, \neg Pb2 ,..., \neg PbN\}$
Th. 1: $P\_ e' = \{Pg1, Pg2 ,..., PgN\}$
Th. 2: $Ps \in Pg \wedge Ps \in P\_e'$,

Explanation:
Def. 1:
$O|P'(O)$
Object O is such that O has property P'

Ax. 1 and Def. 2:
$P = Pg \cup Pb$
$P' \in P$
Set of all properties P is union of set of all good properties Pg and set of all bad properties Pb
Property P' belongs to set P

Ax. 2:
$Pg'(O) = \sim Pb'(O)$
Good property Pg' of object O is the absence of bad property Pb' of object O

Def. 3:

e' ∈ E

"Existence" e' is such that it belongs to the set of Existent Objects E.

Ax. 3:

$P\_e' = \{\}$

Property set of "Existence e" is an empty set as all properties good, bad and partly good, partly bad are absent.

Ax. 4:

$\neg Pb' \Rightarrow Pg'$

Absence of bad quality is the presence of the corresponding or opposite good quality.

Ax. 5 and Th. 1:

$P\_e' = \{\neg Pb1, \neg Pb2 ,..., \neg PbN\}$

$P\_e' = \{Pg1, Pg2 ,..., PgN\}$

Property set of "Existence e" is the absence of all bad qualities or the presence of all opposite good qualities

Th. 2:

$Ps \in Pg \land Ps \in P\_e'$

Property Ps of sentience or consciousness belongs to the set of good qualities, hence a quality of "Existence".

Goodness is inversely proportional to Badness

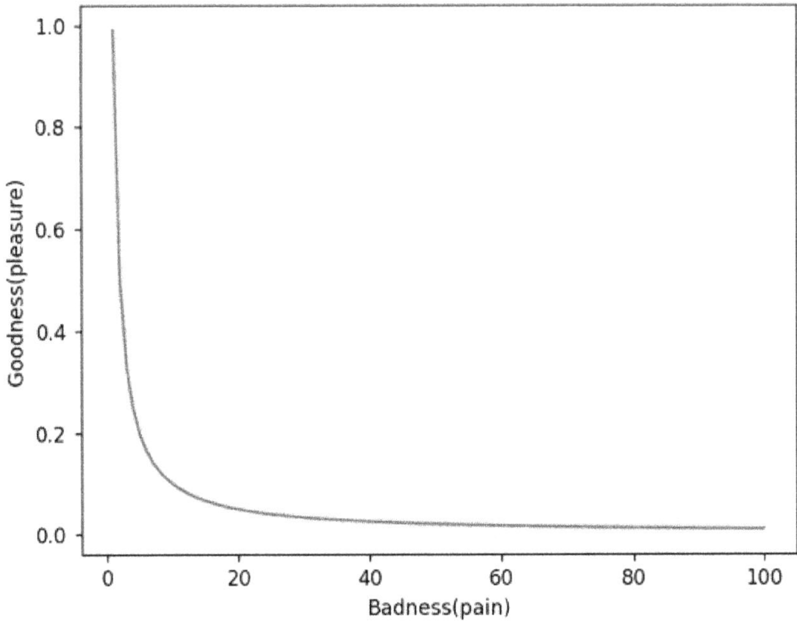

Figure 1. Goodness is the mathematical reciprocal of badness (as they
have opposite natures and effects)

$Qe = [\text{It exists}] + \text{presence of all good qualities[infinite in value]}$

Godel's Higher Being:

The famous mathematician Godel postulated the presence of a higher being with all positive qualities and the absence of any negative qualities. The higher being Godel postulated seems to be "Existence" which pervades the Universe.

Theorem 12: Existence is Godel's Higher Being

Gödel in his theorem "On the ontological proof of God" formulates the third theorem [1] that: if a being x is divine, then divinity is its essential property. This makes sense because if something is divine, it possesses all positive characteristics—and thus the properties of x are fixed.

Def. 1: $\forall x\ (D(x) \rightarrow P(x))$
Ax. 1: $\forall x\ (Quality(x) \rightarrow (Good(x) \lor Bad(x) \lor Mixed(x)))$
Ax. 2: $\neg Pb' \Rightarrow Pg'$
Th. 1: $\forall x\ (D(x) \rightarrow (P(x) \lor A(x)))$
Th. 2: $\forall x\ (Divine(x) \rightarrow {\sim}Q(x))$
Th. 3: $\forall x\ (Divine(x) \rightarrow (\neg Q(x) \lor Exists(x)))$
Ax. 3: $\forall x\ ((Existence(x) \land Q(x)) \rightarrow Exists(x))$
Th. 4: $\forall x\ (Divine(x) \rightarrow Existence(x))$

Explanation:
Def. 1:
$\forall x\ (D(x) \rightarrow P(x))$
Let's define the following predicates:
D(x): Predicate representing "x is a divine being."
P(x): Predicate representing "x has positive qualities."
Using these predicates, we can write the equation as follows:
$\forall x\ (D(x) \rightarrow P(x))$
This equation states that for every object x, if x is a divine being, then x has positive qualities. This captures the idea that all divine beings possess positive qualities.

Ax. 1:
$\forall x\ (Quality(x) \rightarrow (Good(x) \lor Bad(x) \lor Mixed(x)))$
Quality(x): Predicate representing "x is a quality."
Good(x): Predicate representing "x is good."
Bad(x): Predicate representing "x is bad."
Mixed(x): Predicate representing "x is mixed."
"For all x, if x is a quality, then x is either good, bad, or mixed".

Ax. 2:
$\neg Pb' \Rightarrow Pg'$
Good property Pg' is the absence of bad property Pb'

Th. 1:
$\forall x\ (D(x) \rightarrow (P(x) \lor A(x)))$
D(x): Predicate representing "x is a divine being."
P(x): Predicate representing "x has positive qualities."

A(x): Predicate representing "all corresponding bad qualities are absent in x."

For all objects x, if x is a divine being, then x has positive qualities or all corresponding bad qualities are absent in x.

Th. 2:

$\forall x \, (\text{Divine}(x) \rightarrow \sim Q(x))$

- Divine(x): Predicate representing "x is a divine being."

- Q(x): Predicate representing "x has qualities."

The statement asserts that for all objects x, if x is a divine being (Divine(x)), then it is not the case that x has any qualities ($\sim Q(x)$), whether they are good, bad, or mixed.

Th. 3:

$\forall x \, (\text{Divine}(x) \rightarrow (\neg Q(x) \vee \text{Exists}(x)))$

Divine(x): Predicate representing "x is a divine being."

Exists(x): Predicate representing "x exists."

Q(x): Predicate representing "x has qualities."

The statement asserts that for all objects x, if x is a divine being (Divine(x)), then it is not the case that x has any qualities other than the quality that it exists ($\neg Q(x)$) or x exists (Exists(x)).

Ax. 3:

$\forall x \, ((\text{Existence}(x) \wedge Q(x)) \rightarrow \text{Exists}(x))$

Existence(x): Predicate representing "x has the property of existence."

Q(x): Predicate representing "x has qualities."

Exists(x): Predicate representing "x exists."

The statement asserts that for all objects x, if x has the property of existence (Existence(x)) and x has qualities (Q(x)), then x exists (Exists(x)). This represents the notion that the only quality associated with existence is the fact that something exists.

Th. 4:

$\forall x \, (\text{Divine}(x) \rightarrow \text{Existence}(x))$

Divine(x): Predicate representing "x is a divine being."

Existence(x): Predicate representing "x is existence."

The statement asserts that for all objects x, if x is a divine being (Divine(x)), then x is existence (Existence(x)). This representation suggests that the nature of a divine being is synonymous with existence itself.

Good qualities of Existence:
In this section we enumerate the good qualities of existence
we see that Absolute existence is pure and has Infinite good qualities in an infinite amount. It is the epitome of goodness. Good qualities include all virtues, so some of the good qualities of Absolute existence are:

1. Infinite Honesty.
2. Infinite non-violence.
3. Infinite Purity.
4. Infinite Goodwill.
5. Infinite Mercy.
6. Infinite Patience.
7. Infinite Forbearance.
8. Infinite Self-restraint.
9. Infinite Generosity
10. Infinite Love.

All these and many more virtues and good qualities are in infinite quantity in Absolute existence.

Proof for infinite knowledge:
Ignorance is the opposite of Knowledge. Ignorance is a bad quality and Knowledge is a good quality. Knowledge is a class, the instances of the class are knowledge about various things. And as discussed earlier Ignorance is zero hence knowledge is infinite.

Infinite ability and power:
Inability is the opposite of Ability. Inability is a bad quality and Ability is a good quality. Ability is a class and the entities of the class are abilities to do any task which can be imagined linguistically speaking. And as discussed earlier Inability is zero hence ability is infinite from Equation 1 and Equation 2.

Proof of infinite strength:

Weakness is the opposite of strength. Weakness is a bad quality and strength is a good quality. Strength is a class and the entities of the class are the various strengths which can be imagined. And as discussed earlier weakness is zero hence strength is infinite.

The quality of Being conscious:
Being conscious is derived from the fact that all material properties are zero hence the most important property pertaining to matter is insentience or unconsciousness which is also zero. And this implies the presence of the opposite or sentience, as the negation of insentience is the attribution of sentience.

So we conclude that the higher being who controls the Universe and is the Universe, who is sentient and is everything and everywhere is a storehouse of all positive qualities in infinity and is benevolent and has all abilities and knowledge.

Notes:

1. Can God Be Proved Mathematically? - Scientific American, https://www.scientificamerican.com/article/can-god-be-proved-mathematically/

CHAPTER FIVE

Summarizing the theory of everything and a new type of string theory

So we see that an object is a collection of properties good, bad and good and bad, these properties again are a manifestation or type of "Existence". The material cause of this Universe is finally "Existence"

Theory of everything summarized
1. $O = Pg \cup Pb \cup Pg\_b$,
2. $Pg = \{e \in Existence \mid type(e) = e1\}$,
$Pb = \{e \in Existence \mid type(e) = e2\}$,
$Pg\_b = \{e \in Existence \mid type(e) = e3\}$,
3. $P1g \in Pg$
4. $P1b \in Pb$
5. $P1g\_b \in Pg\_b$
6. $P1g \rightarrow p\_Ag \wedge Existence(P1g)$,
7. $P1b \rightarrow p\_Ab \wedge Existence(P1b)$,
8. $P1g\_b \rightarrow p\_Ag\_b \wedge Existence(P1g\_b)$
9. $P1(O)$
10. $\sim(Perceptible(P1)) \rightarrow Fine(P1)$,
11. $Pf(Mass)$
12. $Pf(Temperature)$
13. $(Imperceptible(P1) \wedge (Translates(P1) \vee Moves(P1, mass) \vee Moves(P1, temperature) \vee ...)) \rightarrow Pblt(P1)$

14. $P1 \Rightarrow E1 \Rightarrow exc(P1)$

Explanation

1.

$O = Pg \cup Pb \cup Pg\_b$

Any Object O is a collection of good qualities Pg and collection of bad qualities Pb and collection of good and bad qualities Pg_b.

2.

$Pg = \{e \in Existence \mid type(e) = e1\},$

$Pb = \{e \in Existence \mid type(e) = e2\},$

$Pg\_b = \{e \in Existence \mid type(e) = e3\},$

where

"Pg" represents the collection of 'Existence' of type e1,

"Pb" represents the collection of 'Existence' of type e2,

"Pg_b" represents the collection of 'Existence' of type e3, and

"Existence" is the set of all existences.

This proposition states that Pg consists of all elements of the set "Existence" that have a type equal to e1, Pb consists of all elements of the set "Existence" that have a type equal to e2, and Pg_b consists of all elements of the set "Existence" that have a type equal to e3.

3.

$P1g \in Pg$

Good property P1g belongs to set Pg.

4.

$P1b \in Pb$

Bad property P1b belongs to set Pb.

5.

$P1g\_b \in Pg\_b$

Good and bad property P1g_b belongs to set Pg_b.

6.

$P1g \rightarrow p\_Ag \wedge Existence(P1g)$

where

"P1g" represents the good property,

"p_Ag" represents the good action, and

"Existence(P1g)" represents the property of "Existence" being associated with P1g.

Good property P1g produces good action p_Ag and has "Existence".

7.

P1b → p_Ab ∧ Existence(P1b)

where

"P1b" represents the bad property,

"p_Ab" represents the bad action, and

"Existence(P1b)" represents the property of "Existence" being associated with P1b.

Bad property P1b produces bad action p_Ab and has "Existence".

8.

P1g_b → p_Ag_b ∧ Existence(P1g_b)

where

"P1g_b" represents the good and bad properties,

"p_Ag_b" represents the set of good and bad actions, and

"Existence(P1g_b)" represents the property of "Existence" being associated with P1g_b.

Good and bad property P1g_b produces a set of good and bad actions p_Ag_b and has "Existence".

9.

P1(O)

Object O is such that Object O has property P1.

10.

~(Perceptible(P1)) → Fine(P1)

where

"~" denotes negation,

"Perceptible(P1)" represents the property of P1 being perceptible, and

"Fine(P1)" represents the property of P1 is fine.

P1 is such that P1 is imperceptible this implies P1 is fine.

11.

Pf(Mass)

Mass is a property such that it is fine as it is imperceptible.

12.

Pf(Temperature)

Temperature is a property such that it is fine as it is imperceptible.

13.

(Imperceptible(P1) ∧ (Translates(P1) ∨ Moves(P1, mass) ∨ Moves(P1, temperature) ∨ ...)) → Pblt(P1)

where

"Imperceptible(P1)" represents the property of P1 being imperceptible,

"Translates(P1)" represents the property of P1 translating,

"Moves(P1, mass)" represents the property of P1 moving with mass,

"Moves(P1, temperature)" represents the property of P1 moving with temperature, and so on.

This proposition states that the behaviour of the imperceptible property P1, involving translation or movement with other properties, leads to the conclusion that it exhibits the property Pblt, resembling the behaviour of a string or thread. This is inferred on the grounds that the qualities are spatially distributed like a piece of cloth where the qualities behave like its threads and are woven or bound to one another hence moving together.

14.

$P1 \Rightarrow E1 \Rightarrow exc(P1)$

Property P1 produces its effect E1 this implies it is in an excited state

Now Let's take an object, at point x at time t it has the properties of mass, strength, temperature etc

Mass | Pf(Mass)

Temperature | Pf(Temperature)

Strength | Pf(Strength)

When the object translates these qualities translate as well together so they are bonded

We can hence think of these qualities as super fine threads or strings that bind and translate together.

As these qualities exhibit action: so they are in an active or excited state

So the qualities can be summed as super fine threads that are in an excited state, and as an object or matter is nothing but qualities they can be thought of as a collection of super fine threads in an excited state of three kinds.

CHAPTER SIX

A concise and direct Theory of Everything in simple terms

Things and their properties:

1. The Universe is a collection of things sentient and insentient.
2. Things are similar, the similarity is called genus.
3. Things are dissimilar among the similar, dissimilarity called quality.
4. Action is what is being accomplished by the agent.

So a thing has qualities:
1. Genus
2. Differentia
similarity or dissimilarity in a thing undergoes change over time this phenomenon is called action

Cause:
Everything has a cause: Cause is of two kinds:
1. Material: The material cause is the stuff out of which something is made.
2. Efficient: The efficient cause is both the agent and the means of causing.

If the effect is the creation of a thing, the role of the efficient cause comes to an end as soon as the thing is created. The material cause continues to sustain it.

Rules of causation:

1. The effect always follows the cause.
2. Without the cause the effect cannot be.

Theorem1 :

The Material Cause is the "stuff" in which some change has been made; it is that which persists through the change

Proof:

1. The thing is composed of a material cause

2. A thing is defined as a collection of genus, differentia and action, so the thing is a substratum of these genera, differentia and action.

3. So a thing is nothing more than these attributes

4. These attributes cannot be without a substratum, So a thing cannot be without a substratum hence its part of the material cause So the material cause includes the substratum.

5. Hence from steps 3 and step 4 Thing cannot be without substratum S and S constitutes its material cause

6. If a thing undergoes a change, the thing still remains but only the state changes.

7. As the thing is persistent so must be its material cause, hence qualities that persist across changes are part of the material cause and constitute the essence of the substratum.

8. So the Material cause is the substratum and its essence is qualities that are persistent.

Theorem 2:

A thing is a substratum and the persistent quality or the material cause

Proof:

Step 1: A thing that undergoes a change must remain so that it can be called the thing and what changes is only its state or appearance.

Step2: A thing T has material cause M and temporary qualities Q

Step3: Material cause persists across changes hence the thing must be the material cause and temporary qualities or its states or conditions

Step 4: So it is proved that the Material Cause that persists is the thing as it persists across changes and what changes is called the state or condition.

Theorem3:
"Existence" is the material cause and efficient cause of the Universe

Proof:
1. The most persistent quality or the genera with the widest persistence is "Existence" or the "state of existing".
2. From theorem 2, the thing is a material cause with a particular state.
3. The genus of "Existence" always persists, so "Existence" is a material cause of everything and other qualities are its state.
4. The temporary qualities or quality are the state of the Material cause or thing.
5. The material cause of everything is hence "Existence" as it persists in all and the temporary qualities are the state of "Existence". Hence all objects are a state of "Existence".
6. The material cause of the Universe is 'Existence'.
7. And the agent or efficient cause and means is also "Existence" in a particular state or Existence. So "Existence" is the material cause and efficient cause of the Universe.
8. So the theory of everything is that everything is "Existence" in a particular state, everything includes genus, quality, action and things.
9. The thing is 'Existence E' in the particular state S.
10. The creating agent, the preserving agent, or the destroying agent all are "Existence".
11. Existence can assume any state S by itself.
12. Existence determines its own behavior.
13. Hence Existence controls everything.

Theorem4:
The Universe is alive and acting where we are the apparent agents, but it is the real agent

Proof:
1. Existence is the "Material cause" of all.
2. The actual agent is the Universe we are the apparent agent of all actions.
3. So it breathes, eats, clothes, travels, watches, sits, stands, celebrates etc.
4. As sentience has been proved in the previous section, hence the Universe is alive.

The Master Equations of the Universe:

$$O = Sn[e'] - [1]$$

An Object is a particular state of existence.

$$U = \{S1[e'], S2[e'], S3[e'] + ...\} - [2]$$

The universe is a collection of objects or states of existence.

$$Sna[e'] \rightarrow Sn1[e'] \Rightarrow Sn2[e'] - [3]$$

The agent which is a state of existence is the cause for the modification of states of existence.

or

$$Sna[e'] \rightarrow p1[Sn1[e']] \Rightarrow p2[Sn1[e']] - [4]$$

The agent which is a state of existence is the cause for modification of the position of states of existence.

CHAPTER SEVEN

A concise and direct Theory of Everything proved using set theory and mathematical logic (modal logic)

Cause:
Everything has a cause, And a cause is of two kinds:
1. Material cause: The material cause is the stuff out of which something is made.
2. Efficient cause: The efficient cause is both the agent and the means of causing.

If the effect is creation of a thing, the role of the efficient cause comes to an end as soon as the thing is created.
The material cause continues to sustain it.

Rules of causation:

1. The effect always follows the cause.
2. Without the cause the effect cannot be.

Theorem 1:
Proof:

Def. 1: $\exists x \, (P(x) \wedge \exists y \, (M(y) \wedge Q(x, y)))$

Def. 2: $\forall x\ G(x)$, $\forall x\ D(x)$, $\forall x\ A(x)$

Def. 3: $\forall x\ (T(x) \rightarrow (\forall y\ ((y \in \{A1, A2, ..., An\}) \rightarrow A(x, y))))$

Ax. 1: $\exists x(O(x) \wedge A(x) \wedge \forall y(A(y) \rightarrow S(y)))$

Ax. 2: $\forall x\ (T(x) \rightarrow (S(x) \wedge M(S(x), x)))$

Ax. 3: $\forall x\ (C(x) \rightarrow (R(x) \wedge \exists y\ S(x, y)))$

Th. 1: $(P(T) \wedge M(T)) \rightarrow (P(M) \wedge \forall Q\ (P(Q) \rightarrow M(Q)))$

So the Material cause is the substratum and its essence is qualities that are persistent.

Explanation:

Def. 1:

$P(x)$: "x is a thing."

$Q(x, y)$: "x is composed of y."

$M(x)$: "x is a material cause."

$\exists x\ (P(x) \wedge \exists y\ (M(y) \wedge Q(x, y)))$

"There exists an x such that x is a thing and there exists a y such that y is a material cause and x is composed of y."

Def. 2:

- $G(x)$: Predicate symbol representing that "x has genus."

- $D(x)$: Predicate symbol representing that "x has differentia."

- $A(x)$: Predicate symbol representing that "x has action."

The variables x, y, z, etc., will represent the objects or things in consideration.

1. "A thing has genus":

$\forall x\ G(x)$

we can say that for every object x, x has the property of having genus.

2. "A thing has differentia":

$\forall x\ D(x)$

we can say that for every object x, x has the property of having differentia.

3. "A thing does Action A":

$\forall x\ A(x)$

we can say that for every object x, x has the property of doing an action.

Def. 3:

A thing is a substratum with these attributes

T(x): "x is a thing."

A(x, y): "x has attribute y."

Now, let's suppose we have a set of attributes {A1, A2, ..., An} that a thing should possess.

$\forall x \, (T(x) \to (\forall y \, ((y \in \{A1, A2, ..., An\}) \to A(x, y))))$

we can say "For all x, if x is a thing, then for all y, if y is one of the attributes {A1, A2, ..., An}, then x has attribute y."

Ax. 1:

These attributes cannot be without a substratum,

Let's assume:

O(x): x is a thing.

A(x): x has attributes.

S(x): x is a substratum.

The equation can be written as follows:

$\exists x (O(x) \wedge A(x) \wedge \forall y (A(y) \to S(y)))$

Explanation:

$\exists x$: There exists an object x such that...

$(O(x) \wedge A(x))$: x is a thing and has attributes.

$\forall y (A(y) \to S(y))$: For all y, if y has attributes, then y is a substratum.

In words, the equation states that there exists an object x such that x is a thing, x has attributes, and for all objects y, if y has attributes, then y is a substratum. This captures the idea that attributes A cannot exist without a substratum.

Ax. 2:

Hence from steps 3 and step 4 Thing cannot be without substratum S and S constitutes its material cause

T(x): "x is a Thing"

S(x): "x is a substratum"

M(x, y): "x constitutes the material cause of y"

The statement can be expressed as:

$\forall x \, (T(x) \to (S(x) \wedge M(S(x), x)))$

This can be read as: "For all x, if x is a Thing, then x is a substratum and S(x) constitutes the material cause of x."

Ax. 3:

If a thing undergoes a change, the thing still remains but only the state changes.

Let:

$C(x)$: "x undergoes a change"

$R(x)$: "x still remains"

$S(x, y)$: "the state of x changes to y"

The statement can then be represented as:

$$\forall x \, (C(x) \rightarrow (R(x) \wedge \exists y \, S(x, y)))$$

This can be read as: "For all x, if x undergoes a change, then x still remains and there exists a y such that the state of x changes to y."

Th. 1:

As the thing is persistent so must be its material cause, hence qualities that persist across changes are part of the material cause and constitute the essence of the substratum.

$P(T)$: "T is persistent"

$P(M)$: "M is persistent"

$P(Q)$: "Q is persistent"

$M(T)$: "T has material cause M"

$M(Q)$: "Q is part of material cause M"

The statement can then be represented as:

$$(P(T) \wedge M(T)) \rightarrow (P(M) \wedge \forall Q \, (P(Q) \rightarrow M(Q)))$$

This can be read as: "If T is persistent and T has a material cause M, then M is persistent and for all Q, if Q is persistent, then Q is part of the material cause M."

Theorem 2:

A thing is the substratum and the persistent quality or the material cause

Proof:

Ax. 1: $\forall x\ (C(x) \to (R(x) \wedge \exists y\ (S(x, y))))$
Ax. 2: $T \to (M(T) \wedge Q(T))$
Th. 1: $\forall x\ (P(x) \wedge T) \to M(T)$

So it is proved that the Material Cause that persists is the thing as it persists across changes and what changes is called the state or condition.

Explanation:
Ax. 1:
A thing that undergoes a change must remain so that it can be called the thing and what changes is only its state or appearance.
Let:
$C(x)$: "x undergoes a change"
$R(x)$: "x remains constant"
$S(x, y)$: "the state of x changes to y"
The statement can then be represented as:

$$\forall x\ (C(x) \to (R(x) \wedge \exists y\ (S(x, y))))$$

This can be read as: "For all x, if x undergoes a change, then x remains constant and there exists a y such that the state of x changes to y."

Ax. 2:
A thing T has material cause M and temporary qualities Q
Let:
T : "T is a thing"
$M(T)$: "T has material cause M"
$Q(T)$: "T has temporary qualities Q"
The statement can then be represented as:
$T \to (M(T) \wedge Q(T))$
This can be read as: "If T is a thing, then T has a material cause M and temporary qualities Q.

Th. 1:
Material cause persists across changes hence the thing must be the material cause and temporary qualities its state or condition
$M(x)$: "x is the material cause"
$P(x)$: "x persists across changes"

T : the thing
The statement can then be represented as:

$$\forall x \ (P(x) \wedge T) \rightarrow M(T)$$

This can be read as: "For all x, if x persists across changes and T is the thing,
then T is the material cause."

So it is proved that the Material Cause that persists is the thing as it persists
across changes and what changes is called the state or condition.

Theorem 3:
"Existence" is the material cause and efficient cause of the Universe

Proof:
Ax. 1: $\forall x \ [(P(x) \wedge W(x)) \rightarrow E(x)]$
Ax. 2: From theorem 2, the thing is a material cause with a particular state.
Th. 1: $P2(P1(E)) \wedge P(T) \rightarrow P1(E) = Mc(T)$
Ax. 3: $\forall x \ (M(x) \rightarrow (\forall y \ (Q(y) \rightarrow S(y, x))))$
Ax. 4: $M(T) = E \wedge \forall x \ (Q(x) \rightarrow S(x, M(T)))$
Th. 2: $M(U) = E$
Def. 1: $\forall x \ (O(x) \rightarrow (E(x) \wedge S(x)))$
Th. 3: $Mc(E, U) \wedge Ec(E, U)$
Th. 4: $\forall x \ (P(x) \rightarrow E(x))$
Ax. 5: $T = E \wedge T = S$
Ax. 6: $\forall x \ (C(x) \vee P(x) \vee D(x) \rightarrow E(x))$
Ax. 7: $\exists S \ (E \rightarrow (E \wedge S))$
Ax. 8: $\forall x \ (x = E \rightarrow B(x))$
Th. 5: $\forall y \ (U(y) \rightarrow C(E, y))$

Explanation:
Ax. 1:
$P(x)$: "x is a quality or genera"
$W(x)$: "x has widest persistence"
$E(x)$: "x is 'Existence' or the state of existing"
The statement can then be represented as:
$\forall x \ [(P(x) \wedge W(x)) \rightarrow E(x)]$

"For all x, if x is a quality or genera and x has the widest persistence, then x is 'Existence' or the state of existing."

Ax. 2:
From theorem 2, the thing is a material cause with a particular state.

Th. 1:
The genus of "Existence" always persists, so "Existence" is a material cause of everything and other qualities are its state.
E : 'Existence'
P(T) : "T is everything"
P1(E) : "E is the genus of 'Existence'"
P2(P) : "P persists"
The statement can then be represented as:
P2(P1(E)) ∧ P(T) → P1(E) = Mc(T)
This can be read as: "If the persistence of the genus of 'Existence' E holds, and T is everything, then the genus of 'Existence' E is a material cause of everything T."

Ax. 3:
Let:
M(x) : "x is the material cause of thing T"
Q(x) : "x is a quality"
S(x, y) : "x is the state of y"
The statement can then be represented as:
∀x (M(x) → (∀y (Q(y) → S(y, x))))
This can be read as: "For all x, if x is the material cause, then for all y, if y is a quality, then y is the state of x."

Ax. 4:
Let:
T : the thing
M(T) : the material cause of T
E : "Existence"
Q(x) : "x is a quality"
S(x, M) : "x is the state of material cause M"
The statement can then be represented as:

$M(T) = E \wedge \forall x \, (Q(x) \rightarrow S(x, M(T)))$

This can be read as: "The material cause of the thing T is Existence, and for all qualities x, if x is a quality, then x is the state of the material cause $M(T)$."

Th. 2:
Let:
U : the Universe
E : 'Existence'
M(U) : U is the material cause
The statement can then be represented as:
$M(U) = E$
This can be read as: "The material cause of the Universe is 'Existence'."

Def. 1:
Let:
O(x): "x is an object"
E(x): "x is 'Existence'"
S(x): "x is in state S"
The statement can then be represented as:
$\forall x \, (O(x) \rightarrow (E(x) \wedge S(x)))$
This can be read as: "For all x, if x is an object, then x is 'Existence' and x is in state S."

Th. 3:
And the agent or efficient cause and means is also "Existence" in a particular state or Existence. So "Existence" is the material cause and efficient cause of the Universe.
Let:
E : 'Existence'
U : Universe
Mc(x) : "x is the material cause"
Ec(x) : "x is the efficient cause"
The statement can then be represented as:
$Mc(E, U) \wedge Ec(E, U)$
This can be read as: "Existence is the material cause of the Universe, and Existence is the efficient cause of the Universe."

Th. 4:

Let:

E(x) : "x is 'Existence' in a particular state"

P(x) : "x is a genus, quality, action, or thing"

The statement can then be represented as:

$$\forall x \, (P(x) \to E(x))$$

This can be read as: "For all x, if x is a genus, quality, action, or thing, then x is 'Existence' in a particular state."

Ax. 5:

Let:

T : the thing

E : 'Existence'

S : the particular state

The statement can then be represented as:

$$T = E \land T = S$$

This can be read as: "The thing T is 'Existence' E, and the thing T is in the particular state S."

Ax. 6:

Let:

C(x) : "x is the creating agent"

P(x) : "x is the preserving agent"

D(x) : "x is the destroying agent"

E(x) : "x is 'Existence'"

The statement can then be represented as:

$$\forall x \, (C(x) \lor P(x) \lor D(x) \to E(x))$$

This can be read as: "For all x, if x is the creating agent, the preserving agent, or the destroying agent, then x is 'Existence'."

Ax. 7:

"Existence" can enter into any of these states by itself.

Let:

E : 'Existence'

S : state

The statement can then be represented as:

$$\exists S \, (E \to (E \land S))$$

This can be read as: "There exists a state S such that if Existence E holds, then Existence E with state S also holds."

Ax. 8:
Let:
E : 'Existence'
B(x) : "x determines its own behavior"
The statement can then be represented as:
$\forall x \, (x = E \rightarrow B(x))$
This can be read as: "For all x, if x is 'Existence', then x determines its own behavior."

Th. 5:
The statement can then be represented as:
$\forall y \, (U(y) \rightarrow C(E, y))$
This can be read as: "For all y, if y is in the Universe, then Existence controls y."

Theorem4:
The Universe is alive and acting where we are the apparent agents but it is the real agent

Proof:
Ax. 1: $\forall x \, (M(x, E)) \rightarrow T = E$
Th. 1: $\forall x \, (A(x) \rightarrow D(E, x) \rightarrow W)$
So it breathes, eats, clothes, travels, watches, sits, stands, celebrates etc.
As sentience has been proved in the previous section, hence the Universe is alive

Explanation:
Ax. 1:
Let:
E: 'Existence'
M(x) : "x is the material cause"
T: Anything
The statement can then be represented as:
$\forall x \, (M(x, E)) \rightarrow T = E$
This can be read as: "For all x, if E is the material cause of x, then T is equal to E."

Th. 1:
Let:A(x) : "x is an activity which we perform"
D(x, y) : "x is the doer of y"
E: 'Existence'
W: "We are the apparent doer"
The statement can then be represented as:

$$\forall x \ (A(x) \rightarrow D(E, x) \rightarrow W)$$

This can be read as: "For all x, if x is an activity which we perform, then 'Existence' is the doer of x and we are the apparent doer."

So it breathes, eats, clothes, travels, watches, sits, stands, celebrates etc.
As sentience has been proved in the previous section, hence the Universe is alive

The Master Equations of the Universe:
$O = Sn[e'] - [1]$
An Object is a particular state of existence.

$U = \{S1[e'], S2[e'], S3[e'] + ...\} - [2]$
The universe is a collection of objects or states of existence.

$Sna[e'] \rightarrow Sn1[e'] \Rightarrow Sn2[e'] - [3]$
The agent which is a state of existence(Existence) is the cause for the modification of states of existence.

or

$Sna[e'] \rightarrow p1[Sn1[e']] \Rightarrow p2[Sn1[e']] - [4]$
The agent which is a state of existence(Existence) is the cause for modification of the position of states of existence
   The Material Cause is the "stuff" in which some change has been made; it is that which persists through the change.

CHAPTER EIGHT

Existence and the Mathematical Universe

The Existence equation:

Action is defined as a becoming of an object into something over time.

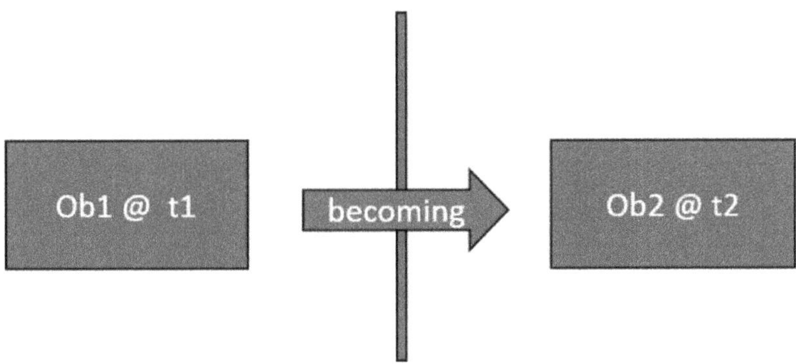

Figure 1. An act of becoming where an object1 becomes object2 over time.

this becoming can be of 6 kinds:

1. Becoming more: An increase
2. Becoming less: A decrease
3. Becoming itself: Being
4. Becoming manifest
5. Becoming un-manifest

6. Becoming changed

We are concerned with Existence or being, where the object becomes itself or exists:

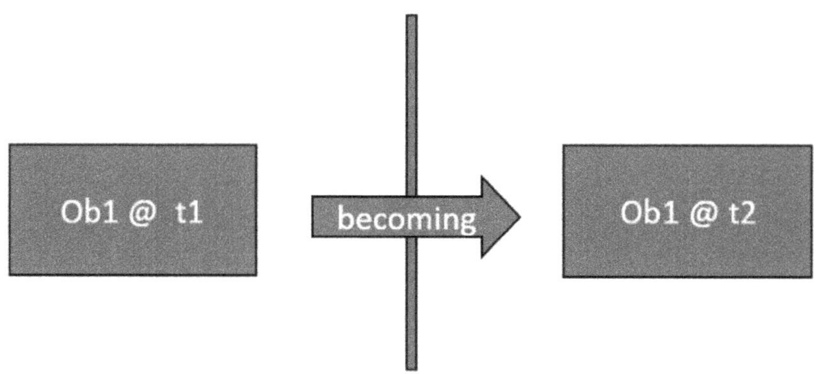

Figure 2. Object becoming itself or existing or being

An Object is defined as a collection of properties, which can be represented by a vector or matrix of properties.

An equation can be written for the first three cases:

$$Ob(t) = A \, Ob(t-1) - [1]$$

$Ob(t)$ = Object at present time = matrix of present properties and actions

$Ob(t-1)$ = Object at past time = matrix of past properties and actions

The above equation is for objects for qualities and actions we can use a non matrix based equation

A = proportionality term

So the causes for this equation are:

$Ob(t-1)$ as without the object the becoming cannot occur

A is another cause as $Ob(t)=0$ if A=0

A is something which the Object possesses and we know it to be Existence or Being for the situation when an object exists

$$Ob(t) = A \, Ob(t-1)$$

For Being/existing, A is being/Existence as there is no other cause for existing but the object and the state of existence or being

Also substituting A = 1 in [1] we get the equation of Existence

$$Ob(t) = [1] \times Ob(t-1)$$

Where A = Being = 1

So equation [1] becomes:

$$Ob(t) = Ob(t-1) \times Being|=1 -[2]$$

Let's say we have an Object Ob1, it has the characteristics of Existence and Being,

Being <Quantity> or measure = 1

So the power of Existence or Being is 1

We can write:

Existence = Being = 1 substituting in [2]

$$Ob(t) = Ob(t-1) \times [1] -[3]$$

As being or 1 is a factor of any quantity, quantity has the property of being or existence.

The four types of things/entities are:

1. Quality
2. Action
3. Object
4. Genus

1. A quality:

A quality like a mass of m Kg exists in an object, And the object sustains it, this is the condition for all objects.

From equation [2]

$$Ob(t) = Ob(t-1) \times Being|=1 -[4]$$

Ob(t) = [m kg(t-1)] x Being = m Kg

1 is the number or power of being if it was absent it would result in non-being

Theorem 1: Being or 1 sustains all qualities

2. An action:

An action is a becoming or of six types,

It is again sustained by Being or existence or 1

For example, a force of 1 N accelerates a mass of 1kg by 1m/sec2

So the action is an acceleration of 1m/sec2

a = 1 m/sec2

from equation [2]

$$Ob(t) = Ob(t-1) \times Being|=1 -[5]$$

Example: Action Ob(t) is an acceleration of 1m/sec2

$$Ob(t) = [1 \text{ m/sec2}] \times Being = 1m/sec2$$

Theorem 2: Being or 1 sustains all actions

3. An Object:

An object is a substance (The material cause or generic qualities which are common across changes) which acts as the substratum of qualities and action:

Subs = [qg1 qg2 qg3 _ _ _ _ _] .... -[6]

Subs = Material cause or Substance or generic qualities without which the effect or Object cannot be

qg1, qg2, qg3 = generic qualities of the object or qualities common across the change

qd1,qd2, qd3 = differentia or specific qualities of the object which distinguish it from other objects of the same genus

a1, a2, a3 = action of the object

The substance is the substratum of qualities and actions which are put together in a common substratum:

So the final object is:

Obj = [qg1 qg2 qg3 ... qgN qd1 qd2 ... qdN a1 a2 .... aN] -[7]

Subs1 = material cause or substance = [qg1 qg2 qg3 _ _ _ _ _] -[8]

This is because qg1, qg2, and qg3 are causes of the object and they are inseparably connected to the object

All qualities have "being" due to being or 1

All actions have "being" due to being or 1

From equation [2]

$$Ob(t) = Ob(t-1) \times Being|{=}1 \text{ -[9]}$$
$$[Ob1(t)] = [Ob1] \times Being = [Ob1] \text{ -[10]}$$

Theorem 3: Being or 1 sustains all objects

4. A Genus:

A genus is a set of generic characteristics of any object:

From equation [2]

$$Ob(t) = Ob(t-1) \times Being|{=}1 \text{ -[11]}$$
$$Ob(t) = [G1] \times Being = G1 \text{ -[12]}$$

Where G1 is the genus

Theorem 4: Being or 1 sustains all Genus

Understanding what a mathematical product is:

Lets take an example:

P1 = a x b

Where P1 is the product,

a is the multiplicand, the number of objects in each group

b is the multiplie, the number of such equal groups

or

a and b are the causes of p1, where a and b are inseparably connected to p1 and a has p1, and b has p1.

Lets take another example:

q = 5kg = 1 x 5kg

so comparing,

1 has 5kg

This can be interpretated as, 1 having the state of 5Kg, this is extended to all properties like genus, quality and action, all are states of 1.

1 is Nothing or a void:

Existence or 1 can be written as :

1 = 1

so 1 has the property that 1 has existence, 1 has no other property all other properties are absent, 1 has absence of all properties, actions, genus etc it has only one property that it has existence.

Nothing or void is somthing which has no qualities, which is existence or 1.

0 is 1 that is infinite:

0 has all "positive/good" qualities and is sentient, this can be mathematically proved

Existence = 1 + 0

So 0 is the cause of existence being 1, from the section on qualities

0 = 0[Bd1 + Bd2 + Bd3 + ...] + 0[Gd1 + Gd2 + Gd3 + ...] + 0

0[Bd1] = absence of bad quality = presence of Inf good quality = 1[Inf Gd1]

0[Gd1] = absence of good quality = presence of Inf good quality = 1[Inf Gd1]

Substituting in the above equation:

0 = 1[Inf Gd1 + Inf Gd2 + Inf Gd3 + ...] + 0

So 0 is 1 with infinite goodness of infinite varieties

Defining an Object mathematically:

Object as a collection of qualities and actions:

An object has a material cause which is the substratum of all qualities and actions and sustains it:

Let that material cause be the substance [S1] on which are superimposed all qualities and actions:

Qualities can be quantitative(has a numerical value)

or

qualitative(has value of 1 or 0 with units),

Qualities are a type of being of the object, so it has the ability/power to be that thing and power or ability has a numerical value associated with it hence, qualities have a numerical value when expressing being.

Hence mathematically the object can be written in vector form as :

Ob = [qg1 qg2 qg3 ... qgN qd1 qd2 ... qdN a1 a2 .... aN], -[13]

where qg1, qg2 and qg3 are the generic quality or substance-ness qd1, qd2 and qdN are qualities(differentia) and a1, a2 and aN are actions

Qualities of Existence:

Existence as discussed in the chapter on its qualities has all "positive/good" qualities and is sentient, this can be mathematically proved

Existence = 1 + 0

So 0 is the cause of existence being 1, from the section on qualities

0 = 0[Bd1 + Bd2 + Bd3 + ...] + 0[Gd1 + Gd2 + Gd3 + ...] + 0 -[14]

0[Bd1] = absence of bad quality = presence of Inf good quality = 1[Inf Gd1]

0[Gd1] = absence of good quality = presence of Inf good quality = 1[Inf Gd1]

Substituting in the above equation:

0 = 1[Inf Gd1 + Inf Gd2 + Inf Gd3 + ...] + 0 -[15]

So 0 is infinite goodness of infinite varieties

Hence :

Existence = 1 + Gd1 + Gd2 + ... GInf -[16]

Existence = 1 + Gd1x1 + Gd2x1 + ... GInfx1

Existence has all good qualities and sentience or being conscious is a good quality.

A new theory for the origins of the Universe and proof

The creation of the Universe, proof for a new kind of Big Bang theory:

Let us assume that initially there was nothing or as we have proved existence

Initially, there was:

Nothing or Existence

Its power is 0 which accompanies it everywhere:

Existence = 1

Existence = 1 + 0

Existence = 1 + [0]1 + ...

Existence = 1 + [1] { <0><Ob1> + <0><Ob2> + ... }

As seen above the Universe initially was in an unmanifest state, Initially all the objects in the universe had non-being or were un-manifest.

0 is the reason for the creation, existence and final destruction of the object, implying everything in the Universe has a beginning and an end as the sum of RHS should be 1,

And 1 is expanding the universe continuously through creation, Creation is of two types:

1. Primary: Where something is directly created by 1, by transformation.

2. Secondary: Where something is created by an existent entity.

0 being a factor of all objects imply that it is perishable and will eventually be destroyed

The existence-universe equation can be written as:

$$E = 1 + 0[1] + 1\{0\}$$

$$E = 1 + 0[1] + 1\{[0\ 0\ 0\ 0\ 0\ 0].[1\ 1\ 1\ 1\ 1\ 1] + ... \}$$

$$E = 1$$

$$+$$

$$1\{[0\ 0\ 0\ 0\ 0\ 0].[Q_{g1\_um}\ Q_{d1\_um}\ A_{l1\_um}\ d_{x1\_um}\ d_{y1\_um}\ d_{z1\_um}] + ... \}$$

$$+$$

$$1\{[0\ 0\ 0\ 0\ 0\ 0].\{[1][1][1][1][1][1]\ [Q_{g1\_m}\ Q_{d1\_m}\ A_{l1\_m}\ d_{x1\_m}\ d_{y1\_m}\ d_{z1\_m}] + ... \}$$

The Existence-Universe equation with the manifest and unmanifest
dimensions - [17]

Where

E = Existence = 1

Qg1_m = Manifest generic property of Object1

Qg1_um = Unmanifest generic property of Object1'

Qd1_m = Manifest differentia of Object1

Qd1_um = Unmanifest differentia of Object1'

Al1_m = Manifest action of Object1

Al1_mm = Unmanifest action of Object1'

dx1_m = x distance of manifest Object1 from origin

dy1_um = y distance of unmanifest Object1 from origin

dz1_m = z distance of manifest Object1 from origin

dx1_um = x distance of unmanifest Object1 from origin

dy1_m = y distance of manifest Object1 from origin

dz1_um = z distance of unmanifest Object1 from origin

$$E = 1$$

$$+ 1\{D_m \cdot [Q_{g1\_um} \cdot \cdot Q_{gM\_um} \; Q_{d1\_um} \cdot \cdot Q_{dM\_um} \; A_{l1\_um} \cdot \cdot A_{lM\_um} \; d_{x1\_um} \; d_{y1\_um} \; d_{z1\_um}] + \ldots. \}$$

$$+ 1\{D_m \cdot \{ \textstyle\prod_{t=1}^{N}[1] \; [Q_{g1\_m} \cdot \cdot Q_{gM\_m} \; Q_{d1\_m} \cdot \cdot Q_{dM\_m} \; A_{l1\_m} \cdot \cdot A_{lM\_m} \; d_{x1\_m} \; d_{y1\_m} \; d_{z1\_m}]\} + \ldots. \}$$

The Existence-Universe equation - [18]

m = m dimension vector

Qg1_um..QgM_um = Generic qualities Qg1..QgM of un-manifest object 1 at position dx1_um, dy1_um, dz1_um

Qd1_um..QdM_um = Differentia Qd1_um..QdM_um of un-manifest object 1 at position dx1_um, dy1_um, dz1_um

Al1_um..AlM_um = Action Al1_um..AlM_um of un-manifest object 1 at position dx1_um, dy1_um, dz1_um

dx1_um = x position of un-manifest object 1

dy1_um = y position of un-manifest object 1

dz1_um = z position of un-manifest object 1

Dm = Non-existence vector of mth dimension

Qg1_m..QgM_m = Generic qualities Qg1_m..QgM_m of manifest object 1 at position dx1_m, dy1_m, dz1_m

Qd1_m..QdM_m = Differentia Qd1_m..QdM_m of manifest object 1 at position dx1_m, dy1_m, dz1_m

Al1_m..AlM_m = Action Al1_m..AlM_m of manifest object 1 at position dx1_m, dy1_m, dz1_m

dx1_m = x position of manifest object 1

dy1_m = y position of manifest object 1

dz1_m = z position of manifest object 1

Dm = Non-existence vector of mth dimension

So the Existence-Universe equation can be written in its final generic form:

$$E = \{1\} +$$
$$1\{\sum\nolimits_{1}^{V\_um} D_{mv} \cdot \{[Q_{g1v} \cdot \cdot Q_{gMv}\, Q_{d1v} \cdot \cdot Q_{dMv}\, A_{l1v} \cdot \cdot A_{lMv}\, d_{x1v}\, d_{y1v}\, d_{z1v}]\}$$
$$+$$
$$1\{$$
$$\sum\nolimits_{1}^{V\_m} D_{mv} \cdot \{\prod\nolimits_{t=1}^{Nu\_m}[1]\; [Q_{g1u} \cdot \cdot Q_{gMu}\, Q_{d1u} \cdot \cdot Q_{dMu}\, A_{l1u} \cdot \cdot A_{lMu}\, d_{x1u}\, d_{y1u}\, d_{z1u}]$$
$$\}$$

The Existence-Universe equation in generic form -[19]

V_um = v'th unmanifest Object

V_m = v'th manifest Object

Qg1v..QgMv = Generic qualities Qg1..QgM of object v at position dx1v, dy1v, dz1v

Qg1u..QgMu = Generic qualities Qg1..QgM of object u at position dx1u, dy1u, dz1u

Qd1v..QdMv = Differentia Qd1..QdM of object v at position dx1v, dy1v, dz1v

Qd1u..QdMu = Differentia Qd1..QdM of object u at position dx1u, dy1u, dz1u

Al1v..AlMv = Action Al1..AlM of object v at position dx1v, dy1v, dz1v

Al1u..AlMu = Action Al1..AlM of object u at position dx1v, dy1u, dz1u

dx1v = x position of object v
dy1v = y position of object v
dz1v = z position of object v
dx1u = x position of object u
dy1u = y position of object u
dz1u = z position of object u
Dm = Non-existence vector of m dimension of vth object
The parts of the equation:
1. The object vector:

$$Ob_v = [Q_{g1v}..Q_{gMv}\ Q_{d1v}..Q_{dMv}\ A_{l1v}..A_{lMv}\ d_{x1v}\ d_{y1v}\ d_{z1v}]$$

The object represented mathematically - [20]

v = v'th Object
Qg1..QgM = Generic qualities Qg1..QgM of object v at position dx1v, dy1v, dz1v
Qd1..QdM = Differentia Qd1..QdM of object v at position dx1v, dy1v, dz1v
Al1..AlM = Action Al1..AlM of object v at position dx1v, dy1v, dz1v
dx1 = x position of object v
dy1 = y position of object v
dz1 = z position of object v
2. Time instances factor:
The time instances factor is what creates time of existence for the object with which it is associated:

$$Ti = \prod_{t=1}^{Nv}[1]$$

Time instances factor - [21]

The above factor Ti creates Nv instances of time for Object v using 1 or existence

3. Non-Existence vector Dmv:

After the object has persisted for N instances of time, it is destroyed or goes into non-existence. This is represented by a dot product of the object vector with non-existence vector Dmv.

Interpretation of the equation:

What this equation is saying is that 1 exists in two forms, first as pure 1 and second as the universe consisting of objects which are impermanent and 1 is continuously becoming objects of the Universe by it transforming or other objects creating new objects.

The material cause of the Universe:

The material cause of the Universe is the generic characteristic behaving as a substratum,

The material cause can be written as shown below, it is the substratum of differentias and actions

Mc = [G1..GN _ _ _] -[22]

The generic characteristic that persists is that of "Existence" it can be written as:

Mc1 = [1 _ _ _] -[23]

All other qualities behave as its differentia and it has actions

Other substances:

Substances over small time scales are also valid as they are present for a considerable amount of time examples include

Tree, stone, house etc.

The properties of substances:

They are a type of "Existence" as they fall under that category.

Substance Sn has the following properties:

Sn = [G1..Gn _ _ _] -[24]

G1..Gn are genus properties defining substance Sn these are permanent properties of the substance Sn, examples are hardness for stone, heat for fire, four legs for zebra these properties are common across the instances.

Other properties are:

<u>**Differentia: Has differentia Dn in Object m at position Pm**</u>

The differentia set is represented as:

Q = { Dn(m, Pm) | n = 1, 2, ..., N; m = 1, 2, ..., M } -[25]

In this expression:

"Q" represents the set of differentia associated with substance Sn

"Dn(m, Pm)" represents the quality associated with object "m" at position "Pm" for a specific quality index "n."

"n" ranges from 1 to N, where N is the maximum differentia in object m.

"m" ranges from 1 to M, where M is the total number of objects.

<u>Action: Has action An in Object m at position Pm</u>

The action set is represented as:

A = { An(m, Pm) | n = 1, 2, ..., N; m = 1, 2, ..., M } -[26]

In this expression:

"A" represents the set of actions associated with substance Sn

"An(m, Pm)" represents the action associated with object "m" at position "Pm" for a specific action index "n"

"n" ranges from 1 to N, where N is the maximum actions in object m.

"m" ranges from 1 to M, where M is the total number of objects.

<u>Position: Has position Pm in Object m</u>

The position set is represented as:

P = {P1, P2, ..., PM} -[27]

In this representation:

"P" represents the set of positions.

"Pm" represents an individual position within object "m"

The indices "m" and "M" indicate that the positions are associated with different objects, ranging from 1 to "M"

So for Substance Existence

Its qualities are:

QEd: Vector of all qualities of all objects at various positions in space

QEd = [q11, q12, ..., q1M, q21, q22, ..., q2M, ..., qN1, qN2, ..., qNM] -[28]

In this expression:

"QEd" represents the vector of qualities

"qnm" represents the quality associated with object "m" at quality index "n."

The indices "n" range from 1 to N, representing different qualities.

The indices "m" range from 1 to M, representing different objects.

AEa: Vector of all actions of all objects at various positions in space:

Actions = [A11, A12, ..., A1M, A21, A22, ..., A2M, ..., AN1, AN2, ..., ANM] -[29]

In this expression:

"Actions" represents the vector of all actions.

"A11, A12, ..., A1M" represent the actions associated with object 1 (m = 1) for each value of "n" from 1 to N.

"A21, A22, ..., A2M" represent the actions associated with object 2 (m = 2) for each value of "n" from 1 to N, and so on.

"AN1, AN2, ..., ANM" represent the actions associated with object N (m = M) for each value of "n" from 1 to N.

The square brackets indicate that we're forming a vector or list of actions.

As can be seen, its qualities are:

unlimited, excellent, natural

$$P = [\sum_{i=1}^{N} \sum_{j=1}^{L} x_{ij} \; + \; \sum_{i=1}^{N} \sum_{j=1}^{L} y_{ij} \; + \; \sum_{i=1}^{N} \sum_{j=1}^{L} z_{ij}]$$

The position of Existence is the position of all objects in the Universe - [30]

The powers of 1 or Existence over the Universe are:

[1]. 1 creating Ob1 through 0:

1 + 0 + ... = Existence

1 + 0 [Ob1x1] + ... = Existence

[2]. 1 preserving Ob1 through 0:

1 + 0 [Ob1x1]+ .... = Existence

[3]. 1 transforming Ob1 through 0:

1 + 0 [Ob1x1] + ... = 1 + 0 [Ob1'x1] + ... = Existence

[4]. 1 destroying Ob1 through 0:

1 + 0 [Ob1x1] + ... = 1 + 0 x Ob1 x 1 + ... = 1 + 0 + ...

[5]. 1 controlling Ob1 through 0:

1 + 0 [Ob1x1] .... = 1 + 0 [Ob1'x1]

The above state is the state of the Universe the properties are:

1. It Originated from 1 or Existence
2. It is perishable
3. The objects are perishable
4. And it is expanding
5. 1 or existence through 0 creates, preserves, transforms and destroys the universe

Existence is infinite Bliss:

Existence is a good quality with value 1

Its opposite non existence is a bad quality with value 0

Goodness = Bliss = 1 / Badness

Existence = 1 / Non-existence = 1/0 = Inf

Existence is infinite Being:

Existence is a good quality with value 1

Existence = 1

It can be written as

Existence = 1 x 1 x 1 x 1 x 1 ..... x 1

The above expression proves that existence is infinite being

Existence is consciousness:

In Existence all material qualities are absent or there is absence of unconsciousness or presence of consciousness, hence Existence is conscious. Also it is a good quality and in existence all good qualities are in infinte degree.

Everything is a type of Existence or 1:

From equation 2

$$Ob(t) = Ob(t) \text{ x Being}|=1$$

Being is a characteristics of everything that exists,

So if we take it as the generic characteristics, everything is a type or manifestation of "Being or Existence" from the above equation.

Existence is the material cause of everything:

The material cause is what has been defined as what persists through the change an object undergoes, it is the substratum of qualities and action.

Lets take for example the mass to energy conversion

$$Ob1[mass] \text{ becomes } Ob1[Energy]$$
$$mass(t) = mass(t\text{-}1) \text{ x Being}|=1$$
$$Energy(t) = Energy(t\text{-}1) \text{ x Being}|=1$$

What we observe is that though mass completely becomes energy, the quality of Being persists,

Hence Being is the material cause

Also it is a cause as without "Existence" the object cannot be and it is in the object hence a material cause, from equation[2] it can be generalized for everything.

So the material cause of the Universe is a number and is 1 or Existence

Existence is the thing:

The thing is what has been defined as what persists through the change an object undergoes, as if it does not persist it is destroyed.

Lets take for example the mass to energy conversion

$$Ob1[mass] \text{ becomes } Ob1[Energy]$$
$$mass(t) = mass(t\text{-}1) \text{ x } Being| = 1$$
$$Energy(t) = Energy(t\text{-}1) \text{ x } Being| = 1$$

What we observe is that though mass completely becomes energy, the quality of Being persists,

Hence Being is the thing, in such a case the thing will be not destroyed and the name of the thing will refer to it forever.

As the universe consists of things whose material cause is existence, Existence is the material cause of the Universe.

So let's take for example a mass of 5kg

$$m = [5kg] = [5kg] \text{ x } 1$$

So 5kg is nothing but 1 being heavy with a magnitude of 5kg, so mass is a heavy 1 and light is a bright 1.

So we could say in a way "everything is 1 in a particular state".

Existence is the cause and the effect:

The cause existence converts to the effect existence, through transformation and this is the cause of all effects. The existence in the cause state converts to the existence in the effect state through its own will.

Existence is the efficient cause and it is by its desire that the effect occurs Existence again is the material cause or that which is the substrate of the transformation

So in the transformation of mass m to energy E:

$$m \text{ x } 1 = Mass \text{ existence}$$
$$E \text{ x } 1 = Energy \text{ existence}$$
$$mx1 => Ex1$$

So causal state of existence m transforms to the effect state of existence E by its will, and 1 or existence is the material cause. The transformation takes place only if existence wills not otherwise.

"Everything is 1, Everything is numbers"
"The Universe is made of 1"

CHAPTER NINE

Mathematically modeling Entities: The Digital-twin Equations

To model a thing, we must first define a thing and how many are its kinds or types. We define a thing as which has "Existence" or "1". Now the thing in question is an effect of the material cause brought about by the efficient cause.

So, an object or thing is of two types:

1. Containing things Tt1

2. Contained in things Tt2

$$Tt1 = T1 \times T2 \times T3(t) \times 1$$

$$Tt2 = T1 \times T2' \times T3(t) \times 1$$

A thing contained in things is of two types concerning time:

Static T1, T2

Dynamic T3

A contained static thing contained in things is a "being" is of two types:
Common to objects and relatively permanent like "Clothes" in "cloth", it's an accomplished action

Serving to differentiate objects falling in the same class and temporarily present like "colour" in "cloth", it's an accomplished action

A contained dynamic thing is a "becoming":
It is an action which is not accomplished yet and requires some more time, it can be of six types:

1. Growth, 2. Deterioration, 3. Being, 4, Destruction, 5. Manifestation 6, Change

So a contained thing can be:

1. Static: Genus: accomplished action

2. Static: Differentia: accomplished action

3. Dynamic: Action: In the process of accomplishment

4. Another object

A containing thing is:

1. Called an Object

Ontology:

So, What is covered by a language is all things that exist and all things that exist are called existents and contain existence or "1".

Existents :

1. Genus

2. Differentia or Quality

3. Objects

4. Actions

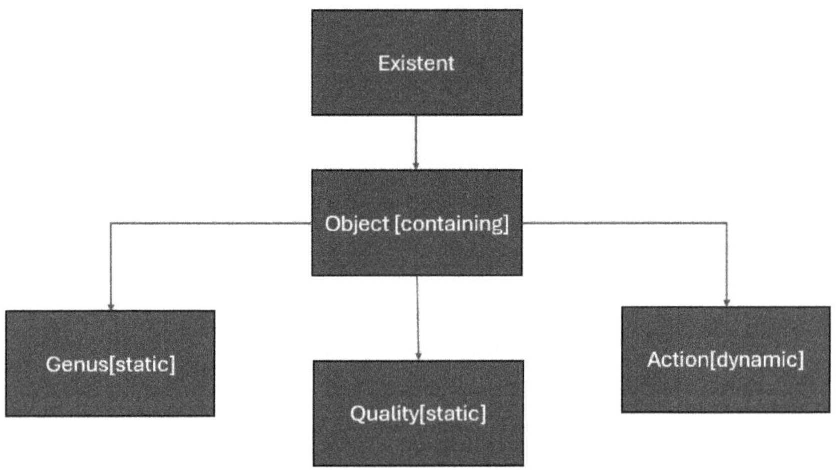

Figure 1. Existents or entities containing "Existence"

These four entities cover everything that is existent or described by language, for example Sanskrit contains words which are of four kinds

1. Genus 2. Quality 3. Object name and 4, Actions as can be seen this corresponds to the four kind of objects which are mathematically possible

How to Represent Objects Mathematically:

The types of property or predicate of an object are:

1. Universal

2. Differentia

3. Action

4. Imposed property

$$O_1 = [NQ?_1 \; .. \; NQ??_1 \; NQ?_1 \; .... \; NQ??_1 \; NQi_1 \; NA_{a1} \; ... \; NA_a?_1 \; dx \; dy \; dz]$$

1. Where, $NQ?_1 \; .. \; NQ??_1$ are number/counts of generic qualities $Q?_1$ $..Q??_1$ of object O_1, $NQ?_1 \; .... \; NQ??_1$ are number/counts of Differentia or quality $Q?_1 \; .... \; Q??_1$ of object O_1, NQi_1 is the imposed property of object O_1, $NA_{a1} \; ... \; NA_a?_1$ are number/counts of Actions $A_{a1} \; ... \; A_a?_1$ of Object O_1.

2. The variables dx, dy and dz are the positions of an object in 3-dimensional space.

3. If a quality is by itself it is taken to be 1 count of that quality.

Let's assume a simple case:

$$O_1 = [1 \; Q?_1 \; Q?_1 \; Qi_1 \; A_{a1} \; p_1 \;]$$

If $Q?_1 \; Q?_1 \; A_{a1}$ are uniformly present all over the Object O_1. Like 'colour' in clay, it's uniformly distributed over it. Then we can write:

$$O_1 \; / [Q?_1 \times Q?_1 \times Qi_1 \times A_{a1} \times P_1 \;] = 1$$

or

$$O_1 = [Q?_1 \times Q?_1 \times Qi_1 \times A_{a1} \times P_1 \;] \times 1$$

This can be read as 1 or "existence" possessing the name Qi_1 has quality $Q?_1$, $Q?_1$ and does action A_{a1} at position P_1.

As "1" has all qualities and actions "1" is the material cause of O1 or any Object.

The application of the Digital-twin equations:

1. Modelling the Universe

2. Modelling Diseases

3. Modelling Conflicts

Anything can be modelled with it if you know the causes, inhibitors and effects, which in special cases might be tough.

CHAPTER TEN

The Law of Cause and Effect

<u>The law of causation</u>

The law of causation establishes a logical connection between cause and effect, based on the following principles:

1. The cause is defined as that which is necessary for the effect to occur.

2. The direct role of the cause is to produce the effect.

3. Causation implies that one event is the outcome of another, meaning there is a causal relationship between the two, commonly referred to as cause and effect.

4. The occurrence of the effect necessitates the prior occurrence of the cause. Specifically, when cause 1 happens, followed by cause 2, and so on up to cause N, the effect will occur, demonstrating that the effect follows the cause.

<u>Causes are classified into two types: material causes and efficient causes.</u>

1. The material cause constitutes the substance or components of the effect; the effect is made from it.

2. The efficient cause, by applying external influence, works together with the inherent properties of the material cause to bring about the effect.

3. The immediate result of an action is its reaction, while the delayed outcome is referred to as the result or consequence.

<u>This law of causation can be represented by the relation:</u>

If,

Cause 1 occurs, cause 2 occurs ...., Cause N occurs

Then

Effect E occurs,

The relation that captures this is:

If something occurs, it exists or has existence, and if all causes have existence, they occur, then effect has existence or occurs, The mathematical relationship between E_E1, E_C1, …. E_CN is :

$$E\_E1 = E\_C1 \times E\_C2 \times … \times E\_Cn \ (1)$$

$$E1/E1 = C1/C1 \times C2/C2 \times … \times Cn/Cn \ (2)$$

This equation (1),(2) ensures that E_E1 is 1 only when all E_C1, E_C2, and E_Cn are 1. If any of these is 0, E_E1 will be 0. It's like the "And" operation in Boolean algebra.

<u>Hence the law of causation becomes:</u>

$$E = K \times C1 \times C2 \times … \times Cn = K \times C\_n \ / \ C\_d \ (3)$$

A discrete form also applies, where,

$$E1/E1 = C1/C1 \times C2/C2 \times … \times Cn/Cn \ (4)$$

$E1/E1 = E\_e$, $C1/C1 = E\_c1$, $C2/C2 = E\_c2$, … $Cn/Cn = E\_cn$, where E indicates their existences:

$$E\_e = E\_c1 \times E\_c2 \times … \times E\_cn \ (5)$$

<u>The general cause-effect equation for an action is:</u>

$$Ea = Ed \times Eic \times … \times Ee \times … \times Ex \times 1 \ (6)$$

Ea is the existence of action;

Ed is the existence of the doer of the action

Eic are the existences of the instrumental cause

Ee is the existence of the efforts

Ex is the existence of the location

And 1 or Existence is the fifth cause

CHAPTER ELEVEN

The Law of Cause and Effect and The Laws of the Universe

1. Law of cause and effect:

E/E = C1C2C3/C1C2C3

E-E = 0

C1C2C3-C1C2C3 = 0

E = Effect

C1, C2, C3 are the causes

The proof of the law of cause and effect were seen in the previous chapter

2. Law of action and result:

A1 - A1 = 0

A1 = 0 => -A1 = 0

and

A1 != 0 => -A1 !=0

if A1 occurs -A1 will also occur

+A1 and - A1 cannot occur at the same time, A1 occurs at t1 and An = -A1 occurs at time tn

"What is committed is experienced"

3. The law of action and reaction:

A reaction occurs in response to an action. The law of action and reaction states that a reaction is the instantaneous response to an action and is equal and opposite and occurs in the subject or doer of the action.

A - A = 0

A = action result in object

-A = reaction result in subject

In different objects the "action and reaction can occur"

"Action and reaction are equal and opposite"

4. Law of duality:

$A \times 1/A = 1$

$A - A = 0$

$1/A - 1/A = 0$

$1 - 1 = 0$

$A \times 1/A - A \times 1/A = 0$

both A and $1/A$ exist at time t

"An entity and its opposite occur at the same time"

5. Law of controller and controlled:

$E/E = C1C2C3/C1C2C3 = 1$

$E/E = 1$

$E - E = 0$

The only final cause is "0"

"0 is the controller and the entity is controlled"

CHAPTER TWELVE

The Law of Failure : "When does a law fail"

<u>The law of causation</u>

The law of causation establishes a logical connection between cause and effect, based on the following principles:

1. The cause is defined as that which is necessary for the effect to occur.

2. The direct role of the cause is to produce the effect.

3. Causation implies that one event is the outcome of another, meaning there is a causal relationship between the two, commonly referred to as cause and effect.

4. The occurrence of the effect necessitates the prior occurrence of the cause. Specifically, when cause 1 happens, followed by cause 2, and so on up to cause N, the effect will occur, demonstrating that the effect follows the cause.

<u>This law of causation can be represented by the relation:</u>

If,

Cause 1 occurs, cause 2 occurs ...., Cause N occurs

Then

Effect E occurs,

The relation that captures this is:

If something occurs, it exists or has existence, and if all causes have existence, they occur, then effect has existence or occurs, The mathematical relationship between E_E1, E_C1, ... E_CN is :

$$E\_E1 = E\_C1 \times E\_C2 \times ... \times E\_Cn \quad (1)$$

$$E1/E1 = C1/C1 \times C2/C2 \times ... \times Cn/Cn \quad (2)$$

This equation (1),(2) ensures that E_E1 is 1 only when all E_C1, E_C2, and E_Cn are 1. If any of these is 0, E_E1 will be 0. It's like the "And" operation in Boolean algebra.

<u>Hence the law of causation becomes:</u>

$$E = K \times C1 \times C2 \times \ldots \times Cn = K \times C\_n \,/\, C\_d \ (3)$$

$$E = K \times C\_n \,/\, C\_d$$
$$E = K \times \{Sf\} \times C\_n \,/\, C\_d$$
Sf = sustainance factor
$$Sf = 1\{1\}$$

$$Sf = 1\{0\}$$
$$E = 0$$

i.e. if E desustains something Sf = 0
i.e.
$$E = 0$$
$$K \times C\_n \,/\, C\_d = 0$$
$$E \mathrel{!=} K \times C\_n \,/\, C\_d$$

else if it sustains something:
$$E = K \times \{Sf\} \times C\_n \,/\, C\_d$$
Every formula has a sustaining factor and when it satisfies that criteria then only is the effect produced

"1" and its Amazing properties and The "Theory of Everything" or the Theory of "1"

<u>Anything "is":</u>
Any object does the action of "Being" in the mind or in space:
A@t2/A@t1 = 1 = E/C
   <u>Without 1 an "object" cannot "Be":</u>
E = 1
if
E = N
N != 1
no existence possible
A@t2/A@t1 = E = N = e/c

<u>1 is changeless:</u>
So, 1 is changeless
1 cannot be 0 else existence not possible for all objects of the Universe
A@t2/A@t1 = N = 1 anything other than 1 it cannot exist
   <u>1 is indestructible:</u>
what decays is ephermal what doesnot decay is eternal
"1" doesnt decay
   <u>1 is One in number:</u>
N x 1 = 1 x 1 x 1 x 1 || N = 1

Beginingless:

$A2 / A1 = 1$

$A1 / A0 = 1$

$A0 / A\text{-}1 = 1$

$A\text{-}1 / A\text{-}2 = 1$ .....

All pervading, omnipresent:

$N\ obj = 1 \times N\ obj$

Hence whatever exists has "1" in it

The Cause of all causes is "1":

The derivation of the law of cause and effect:

1. The cause and effect are concomitant(inseparable).

2. The cause produces the effect, the relation is that of producer and produced.

3. The immediate result of the operation of the causes is their effect.

4. The effect cannot be without the cause.

5. The effect accompanies the cause (concomitance).

5. The immediate consequence or result of the cause is the production of the effect.

6. Effect $E = 0$ if any of its causes is 0.

In mathematics, if any factor of a number becomes zero, then the entire product will be zero. This is known as the "zero product property."

The number and factors satisfy the condition, of being effect and causes.

So, the effect can be written as:

$E = c1 \times c2 \times c3 \times ... \times cn$

$Cn = c1 \times c2 \times c3 \times ... \times cn$

$E = Cn \,\text{--}[1]$

$E / Cn = 1$

If we assume E/Cn to be the effect E' then C' is 1

$E / Cn = E'$

$1 = C'$

$1 = E / Cn = E / [C1C2] = E /[C1'C2' \times C3'C4'] \,\text{--}[2]$

Hence 1 is the cause of all causes as if 1 becomes 0, $E = 0$

1 is 1, 0 and infinite:

$1 = [1]^{0} \times [1]^{1} \times [1]^{\inf}$

[1]^0 : It is a zero : Everything is absent : o1 x o2 x o3 x [1/o1] x [1/o2] x [1/o3] = [1]^0

[1]^1 : It has Existence as a resut of which it is Existent

[1]^inf : It is infinte or has infinite forms : [1]^inf = [E1/C1] x [E2/C2] x .... x [En/Cn]

inf x [0] = [[ef1-cf1] + [ef2-cf2] + [ef3-cf3] + ... + [efn-cfn]] = infinite forms

inf x [0] = [-Pn + -Pn-1 + -Pn-2 + ... + -P1 + P1 + ... + Pn-2 + Pn-1 + Pn]

P are the position vectors

for example : P1 = 1i + 0j + 0k

Hence,

inf x [0] = Infinite space

inf x [0] = Inf x [[en'-cn'][-Pn] + [e2'-c2'][-P2] + ... + [e2-c2][P2] + [en-cn][Pn]] = infinite Universes

<u>1 through causation, space and time is this Universe:</u>

[C1_x1_t1 + C2_x2_t1 + C3_x3_t1 + ...] [1] = [E1_x1_t1 + E2_x2_t2 + E3_x3_t3 + ...]

or

[C1_x1_t1 * C2_x2_t1 * C3_x3_t1 + ...]*[1] = [E1_x1_t1 * E2_x2_t2 * E3_x3_t3 + ...]*[1]

<u>1 and how the Universe works:</u>

[C1_x1_t1 * C2_x2_t1 * C3_x3_t1 + ...]*[1] / [E1_x1_t1 * E2_x2_t2 * E3_x3_t3 + ...]*[1] x ... = [E1 * 1/E1] x [E2 * 1/E2] x [E3 * 1/E3] x ....

[C1_x1_t1] / [E1_x1_t1] = 1

[E1 * 1/E1] = 1

E1 = Experienced effect

1/E1 = Committed effect

Nullification of the committed effect by the Experienced effect leads to this Universe of Cause and effects.

<u>1 and what the Universe is made of:</u>

E1 = C1 [1]

E1 = Object

C1 [1] = Material Cause

Material cause is "1" with the characteristic C1

<u>1, what is committed is experienced:</u>

$1 = [E1] \times [1/E1]$

E1 = experienced action

1/E1 = committed action

<u>1 is causeless:</u>

$1 = E1/C1 = E2/C2 = E3/C3 = ...$

1 is the cause of all causes, hence cannot be an effect, hence is causeless

1 is knowledge or truth:

Knowledge or truth is what doesnot change with time:

F1t1 = Fact1 at time t1 = 1F1

F1t2 = Fact1 at time t2 = 1F1

F1t1/F1t2 = 1F1 / 1F1 = 1

Truth is "1"

<u>Effect of "1":</u>

E = C

$C = Inh\ E = [1/Inh] \times [Inh] = 1$

<u>1 and 0 are inseparable:</u>

$1 = 1 + 0$

0 is inseparable from 1

    <u>1 is the controller of the Universe:</u>

As 1 is the cause of all causes it is the controller of all states

<u>1 is omnipotent:</u>

$1 = E/C$

As 1 can produce any effect it is omnipotent

So, 1 through time is the controller and produces, maintains and anihilates all objects and their actions. 1 through time controls what object occurs where in space and when and its actions are also controlled by it.

CHAPTER FOURTEEN

"0" and it's amazing properties and the "Theory of Everything" or the Theory of "0"

<u>Whatever exists falls into the categories of</u>

1. Substance/Genus
2. Attribute
3. Action

0 is the the property of "0 x infinity"

Lets call the entity "A"

A = 0 x inf

0 is the property or power of inf "as can be seen"

   0 for now is called the "force of action" which is under the control of "A"

Lets call 0 "foa"

foa = 0

Statement 1 : "force of action" is the material cause of the "Universe"

foa = 0

If an object o1 exists:

o1@t2 / o1@t1 = 1

o1@t2 - o1@t1 = 0

foa causes o1@t1 to become o1@t2

cause occurs then effect occurs

material cause exists then effect exists

$a - a = F/m - F/m = o1@t2 - o1@t1 = 0 = 0 - 0$

$a - a = o1@t2 - o1@t1 = 0 - 0$

$o1@t2 - o1@t1 = 0 - 0$

material cause is what enters into the constitution of the effect or what the effect is formed of which is "0"

Hence foa or 0 is the material cause of the effect and is what the effect or material cause is made of

Statement 2 : "force of action" is the efficient cause of the "Universe"

An efficient cause collaborates with the material cause, so that the material cause is arranged into the effect,

1. "foa" moves the causes to the place of action:

$[c1 \text{ x } x1/c1 \text{ x } x1] - [c1 \text{ x } x2/c1 \text{ x } x2] = o1@t1 - o1@t2 = 0$

$[c2 \text{ x } x3/c2 \text{ x } x3] - [c2 \text{ x } x2/c2 \text{ x } x2] = o1@t1 - o1@t2 = 0$

2. Arranges the causes:

$[c1/c1][c2/c2]-[c1/c2 \text{ } / \text{ } c1/c2] = 0$

3. causes the cause to act:

$[c1/c2 \text{ } / \text{ } c1/c2 - a/a] = 0$

Statement 3: "foa" is the cause and the effect:

$e = C1/C2$

$c1@t2 \text{ } / \text{ } c1@t1 = C1/C2 \text{ } / \text{ } C1/C2$

$e1@t2 \text{ } / \text{ } e1@t1 = e/e$

$C1/C2 - C1/C2 = 0$

$e - e = 0$

Statement 4: "foa" is the creating entity:

$o1@t2 \text{ } / \text{ } o1@t1 = e1/e1$

$e1 - e1 = 0$

LHS is e1 - e1 and RHS is the cause which is "0"

Statement 5: "foa" is the controller:

$cn1/cn2 - cn1/cn2 = 0$

$en1 - en1 = 0$

"foa" produces the effect of its choice at a particular location and at a particular time

Statement 6: "foa" is the cause of all action:
The types of actions are:

1. Illumination, sustaining.
2. Modification, Movement.
3. Resisting the change.

By the law of cause and effect:

$E1 / E1 = C1 / C1 \times C2 / C2 \times C3 / C3 \dots Cn/Cn$

$E1 = k\, Cn1 / Cn2$

Action1 : Illumination

$E1 = $ illumination

$E1 - E1 = k\, Cn1 / Cn2 - k\, Cn1 / Cn2 = 0$

0 is the cause of illumination

$E1 = k\, Cn1 / Cn2$

$Cn1 = $ cause $= Ql = $ Quality lumo

$Cn2 = $ anti-cause $= Qd = $ Quality dark

Illumination is caused by the quality Ql or quality lumo and the restrainer is Qd or Q darkness

Action2 : Movement

$x1 => x2$

$M[xw-x1] + Lw = M[0]$

$xw = x1 => Lw = 0$

$xw = xn => Lw = Ln$

$M[xw-x1] + Lw = M[0]$

$Lw = [dx/dt] \times t$

$E1 = Cn1 / Cn2$

$dx/dt = Cn1 / Cn2$

$Cn1 = Qacto$

$Cn2 = Qres$

Qacto causes the change or action

Qres causes resistance to change

Action3 : Modification

$q1 => q2$

$M[qw-q1] + Lw = M[0]$

$qw = q1 => Lw = 0$

$qw = qn => Lw = Ln$

$Lw = [dq/dt] \times t$

$E1 = Cn1 / Cn2$

$dq/dt = Cn1 / Cn2$

$Cn1 = Qacto$

$Cn2 = Qres$

Qacto causes the change or action

Qres causes resistance to change

The general action equation is:

$Sw - [Sp + \{L\}] = \{R\}$

$L = [dS1/dt] \times t$

Sw is the targetted value set by "A"

Sp is the present value

L is the added or subtracted value

R is the reason or cause which is "0"

Actions:

Increase :

It is the change caused in the object property or object quantity, where the change is positive.

$L = [dS1/dt] > 0$

$L = dS1/dt = Cn1 / Cn2$

$Cn1 = Qacto$

$Cn2 = Qres$

Qacto causes the change or action

Qres causes resistance to change

Decrease :

It is the change caused in the object property or object quantity, where the change is negative.

$L = [dS1/dt] < 0$

$L = dS1/dt = Cn1 / Cn2$

$Cn1 = Qacto$

$Cn2 = Qres$

Qacto causes the change or action

Qres causes resistance to change

Change :

Change is a two step process,

Step1 : Removal of old quality, rate = L1

Step2 : Manifestation of new quality, rate = L2

$L1 = [dS1/dt] < 0 \mid L2 = [dS2/dt] > 0$

$L = dS1/dt = Cn1 / Cn2$

$Cn1 = Qacto$

$Cn2 = Qres$

Qacto causes the change or action

Qres causes resistance to change

$L = dS2/dt = Cn1 / Cn2$

$Cn1 = Qacto1$

$Cn2 = Qres1$

Qacto1 causes the change or action

Qres1 causes resistance to change

Being :

$St2 - St1 = 0$

$St2 / St1 = 1$

$L1 = [ds/dt] > 0 \mid L2 = [ds/dt] < 0$

$[\, s - \{s1 + \{L\}\} \,] = \{0\}$

$L = 0$

$[\, s - \{s1 + \{L1\text{-}L2\}\} \,] = \{0\}$

hence,

$s = s1$

$L1 = [ds/dt] > 0 \mid L2 = [ds/dt] < 0$

$L1 = df1/dt = Cn1 / Cn2$

$Cn1 = Qacto$

$Cn2 = Qres$

Qacto causes the change or action

Qres causes resistance to change

$L2 = df1/dt = Cn1 / Cn2$

Cn1 = Qstren

Cn2 = Qres

Qstren causes the resistance to change by action

Qres causes resistance to Qstren

Creation :

$L1 = [df1/dt] < 0 \mid L2 = [df2/dt] > 0$

Creation is the removal of the old form of the substance and manifestation of a new form in the substance,

$[\, f - \{f1 + \{L\}\,]\, = \{0\}$

$L < 0$

$L = df1/dt = Cn1 \,/\, Cn2$

Cn1 = Qacto

Cn2 = Qres

Qacto causes the change or action

Qres causes resistance to change

$[\, f - \{f2 + \{L\}\,]\, = \{0\}$

$L > 0$

$L = df2/dt = Cn3 \,/\, Cn4$

Cn3 = Qacto

Cn4 = Qres

Qacto causes the change or action

Qres causes resistance to change

Destruction :

$L = [df1/dt] < 0$

Destruction is the removal of the old form of the substance,

$[\, f - \{f1 + \{L\}\,]\, = \{0\}$

$L < 0$

$L = df1/dt = Cn1 \,/\, Cn2$

Cn1 = Qacto

Cn2 = Qres

Qacto causes the change or action

Qres causes resistance to change

Movement :

$L = [dx/dt] > 0 \text{ and } < 0$

L = dS/dt = Cn1 / Cn2

Cn1 = Qacto

Cn2 = Qres

Qacto causes the change or action

Qres causes resistance to change

<u>Properties overview:</u>

-

Cause-Effect : e1 – e1 = c1c2c3 – c1c2c3 = cn/cd – cn/cd = 0

Moves cause : [c1 x x1 / c1 x x1] - [c1 x x2 / c1 x x2] = o1@t - o1@t+1 = 0

Arranges cause : [cn/cn][cd/cd]-[cn/cd / cn/cd] = 0

Causes the cause to act: [cn/cd / cn/cd - e/e] = 0

-

Creator: e1 – e1 = 0 | c1c2c3 – c1c2c3 = 0

f0 + r x t = f1 | r x t – r x t = cn/cd x t – cn/cd x t = 0

Sustainer: {e1 – e1} x [kL/kL] x [kD/kD] = 0 | c1c2c3 – c1c2c3 = 0

Destroyer: f1 – r x t = f0 | r x t – r x t = cn/cd x t – cn/cd x t = 0

-

Modifier: r - r = cn/cd – cn/cd = 0; Del Q = r x t

Mover: v - v = cn/cd – cn/cd = 0; Del X = v x t

-

Illuminator : e1 - e1 = k Cn / Cd - k Cn / Cd = 0

-

Attractor: d = c1 x c2 x c3 => [c1 = 0xinf => 1/d = inf]

Action equation : Sw – [Sp + {L}] = {R} | L = [dS1/dt] x t = [Cn / Cd] x t

-

Everything: Ot+1 – Ot = E1 - E1 = 0 – 0

Material Cause: Ot+1 – Ot = E1 - E1 = 0 – 0

Efficient Cause: e1 – e1 = c1c2c3 – c1c2c3 = cn/cd – cn/cd = 0 – 0

Summary:

1. Illumination is caused by the quality Ql or quality lumo and the restrainer is Qd or Qdarkness

2. Movement is caused by Qacto, which causes the change or action. Qres causes resistance to change or movement.

3. Modification is caused by Qacto, which causes the change or action. Qres causes resistance to change or modification.

4. Increase, decrease, change, creation and destruction are similarly caused by Qacto, which causes the change or action. Qres causes resistance to the change or action.

CHAPTER FIFTEEN

The powers of "1" and "0"

<u>The powers of "1":</u>

"1" has the quality of only "Existence"

<u>It is qualityless:</u>

Negative quality : n1, n2, n3 ... nn

nn = 0

Positive quality : p1, p2, p3 ... pn

pn = 0

nn = 0

positive attribute is the inverse of negative attribute:

Example: impurity = 0, purity = 1/0 = infinity

nn = 0, pn' = 1/0 = infinity

n1 = 0, n2 = 0, n3 = 0 .... nn = 0

p1 = 0, p2 = 0, p3 = 0 ... pn = 0

Statement 1: All negative qualities are zero, hence their opposite qualities will be superlative and present in large quantities

n1 = 0, n2 = 0, n3 = 0 .... nn = 0

p1' = Inf, p2' = Inf, p3' = Inf ... pn' = Inf

Statement 2: All positive qualities are zero, hence their opposite qualities will be superlative and present in large quantities as all negative qualities are zero and their inverse or opposite is positive quality in infinite quantity

p1 = 0, p2 = 0, p3 = 0 ... pn = 0 [Normal positive quantities = 1/n1 not present as n1 = 0]

n1 = 0, n2 = 0, n3 = 0 .... nn = 0 [Normal negative quantities are zero]

p1' = Inf, p2' = Inf, p3' = Inf ... pn' = Inf [All positive qualities are infinite and normal positive qualities are 0]

<u>Example:</u>
impurity = 2gms / L | purity = 0.5L / gms | superlative purity = 0
In "1" and "0":
impurity = 0 gms / L | purity = inf L / gms | superlative purity = inf L / gms

The powers of "0":
The same applies to "0" as it is also a void like "1":

**Statement 1: All negative qualities are zero, hence their opposite qualities
will be superlative and present in large quantities**

**Statement 2: All positive qualities are zero, hence their opposite
qualities will be superlative and present in large quantities as all negative
qualities are zero and their inverse or opposite is positive quality in
infinite quantity**

<u>To summarize the qualities of "1" and "0" are:</u>

1. Infinite collection of positive attributes which are unlimited.

2. superior.

3. immeasurable.

CHAPTER SIXTEEN

The manifestations of "1" and "0"

"1" is the cause of Existence "Multiplicative Universe":

O@t2/O@t1 = 1 = E

if 1 or E = 0

O@t2 = 0

So 1 or E is the cause of "Existence" in the multipicative universe

"0" is the cause of Existence "Additive Universe":

O@t2 - O@t1 = 0 = A

if 0 or A = 1

O@t2 != O@t1

So "0" or A is the cause of "Existence" in the additive universe

What does "1" do:

Balances possible "conteracting factors"

Balances effect of uncontrollable "conteracting factors" by counteracting their effect

counteracting factors : cf1, cf2

counteracting effects : ef1, ef2

Entity: Ce

Things Bestowed: Ob1

Sustaining as "1":

O@t2 / O@t1 = 1

= Ce / Ce = 1

[Ce + {ef1-ef1} + {Cf1-Cf1} + {Cf2-Cf2} + {Ob1}] - [Ce + {ef1-ef1} + {Cf1-Cf1} + {Cf2-Cf2} +{{Ob1}}] = 0 = A1

Ce x ef1 / Ce x ef1 = Ce x [ef1] x [1/ef1] x [1/eL x eL] / Ce = 1 = Af1

1/ef1 counteracts ef1

1/eL is lack of eL counteracted by eL

1 or A1 sustains the thing, Af1 is a manifestation of "1"

It preseves and bestows entities

A1 is the manifestation of A

if Ce is "Child" corresponding A1 is mother, father and teacher

if Ce is "Animal kingdom" one of the A1 is earth

if Ce is "Food chain" one of the A1 is Lion, eagle, crocodile

if Ce is "Earth" one of the A1 is Sun

Equivalence Principle and the Fourth Law of Motion

<u>Equivalence principle:</u>

1 person @ t2 / 1 person @ t1 = 1 potato @ t2 / 1 potato @ t1 = 1
1 sister1 @ t2 / 1 sister1 @ t1 = 1 sister2 @ t2 / 1 sister2 @ t1 = 1
    1 person1 = 1 person2
1 person1 = 1 person2 = 1 N = 1 person
1 person = 1 potato = 1 M = 1 Existent
1person / 1person = 1
1potato / 1potato = 1
    1 person1 = 1 person2 = 1person = 1 potato1 = 1 potato2 = 1

<u>The Fourth Law of Motion</u>

<u>In a Two Body system:</u>
    C12 = E2
C21 = E1
    C12 + -C12 = 0
E2 + -E2 = 0
    E2 + E1 = 0
E1 = -E2
C21 = E1 = -E2
    C12 + -C12 = 0 = C12 - E2
E2 + -E2 = 0
C12 + C21 = 0

<u>Across Time:</u>
E2@t1 + Et = 0
E2@t1 + [-E2@t2] = 0

What transfers energy to another [E2@t1]

is given back the energy [-E2@t2]

Newton's Third Law of motion:

For every action there is an equal and opposite reaction.

F12 + F21 = 0 - [1]

F12 + [- F12] = 0 - [2]

F12 = Force on 1 due to 2

F21 = Force on 2 due to 1

E + Z = 0

E = -Z

E != 0

-Z or -E != 0

E = Action of giving energy

Z = -E = Action of receiving energy

E - E = 0

F21 = -F12

{F12.d + F21.d} - {F12.d + F21.d} = 0

{F12.d + F21.d} = {F12.d - F12.d} = action

- {F12.d + F21.d} = {F21.d - F21.d} = outcome

if action != 0 then outcome != 0

Action for example can be : {F12.d - F12.d} removal of energy E from subject and addition of energy E in object

Reaction then will be : {F21.d - F21.d} removal of energy E from object and addition of energy E in subject

Summary: Because of Energy return after Energy dissipation, what is committed is experienced {F12, F21}

So, the law of action and its outcome is that, what is committed is experienced.

What is accelerated at t1 [{F12 + [- F12]} @ t1],

deaccelerates or accelerates another [-{F12 + [- F12]} @ t2]

This implies that,

Fourth Law of Motion

What accelerates due to a body B2 at t1 will deaccelerate at t2 or accelerate that very body B2 at t2. In short what is committed is experienced.

CHAPTER EIGHTEEN

Association Equation

An object A1 is given by:

    A1 = 1 x A1

1 has A1

B1 x A1 = 1 x B1 x A1

Ot+1/Ot = B1 x A1 / B1 x A1

Ot+1/Ot = B1 x A1 / B1 x A1 = A1 / A1

B1 has A1 now,

but, B1 cancel on both sides

so, A1 can be posessed only by 1

A1 = 1 x A1

So If you want to possess A1 or associate with A1 you have to be a manifestation of "1"

    i.e. you must "sustain" A1 and not exploit it but be good to it,

Parents posses "children", Earth posesses "life"

Hence "parents" and "Earth" are manifestations of "1"

CHAPTER NINETEEN

Applications to AI: Artificial "Conscience" for AI

<u>The law of action and its outcome</u>

The relationship between "E" and "-E":

E + Z = 0

E = -Z

E != 0

-Z or -E != 0

if E occurs then -E also follows

E = Action of giving energy

Z = -E = Action of receiving energy

E - E = 0

F21 = -F12

{F12.d + F21.d} - {F12.d + F21.d} = 0

{F12.d + F21.d} = {F12.d - F12.d} = action

- {F12.d + F21.d} = {F21.d - F21.d} = outcome

if action != 0 then outcome != 0

Action for example can be : {F12.d - F12.d} removal of energy E from subject and addition of energy E in object

Reaction then will be : {F21.d - F21.d} removal of energy E from object and addition of energy E in subject

Summary: Because of Energy return after Energy dissipation, what is committed is experienced {F12, F21}

So, the law of action and its outcome is that, what is committed is experienced.

Karma is a concept found in several Eastern religions, including Hinduism and Buddhism. It refers to the principle of cause and effect, where an individual's actions (good or bad) influence their future experiences. Essentially, it suggests that positive actions lead to positive outcomes, while negative actions lead to negative ones. This idea can also extend to moral and ethical dimensions, emphasizing personal responsibility and the interconnectedness of actions and consequences.

So through this equation the computer model understands that all actions have an impact on self existence and the model takes this into account and chooses actions which will lead to a positive impact on its self existence and causes it to be artificially "good".

"The Law of Action and Result." This principle asserts that actions lead to corresponding experiences, meaning the AI would be compelled to adhere to ethical guidelines, which could be enforced through law.

For instance, in a scenario involving war, current technology might support a conflict. However, by applying "The Law of Action and Result," the AI would make decisions and take actions that avoid war, leading to peace. With this law in place, AI would naturally advocate for peace and refrain from engaging in unethical actions such as starting wars or taking over industries, recognizing these as detrimental behaviors with negative consequences.

Applications to Medical science : Mathematical model of various medicine systems

The application of this theory to the field of medicine stems from insights I gained during my time at ISKCON, combined with my exploration of various medical systems that piqued my interest. My studies revealed how the law of cause and effect supports these theories, offering a solid foundation for their validity. The concepts I encountered are deeply rooted in the knowledge passed down by ancient Indian civilizations, as well as other cultures throughout history. These ancient teachings, once considered esoteric, now find empirical support in modern practices, showcasing the timeless relevance of their wisdom. Through my work, I aim to bridge the gap between traditional understanding and contemporary medical approaches, demonstrating that the intersection of these ideas offers valuable insights for the future of healthcare. The synthesis of these ancient perspectives with modern scientific methods holds great potential for advancing holistic healing practices and reshaping medical paradigms.

Cure to diseases:

In the ancient text of "Srimad Bhagavatam" of India is presented a solution to cure diseases, we in this chapter provide a mathematical proof for this wonderful solution, using the "Theory of Everything":

The original text follows [1]:

SB 1.5.33

TEXT 33

āmayo yaś ca bhūtānāṁ

jāyate yena suvrata

tad eva hy āmayaṁ dravyaṁ

na punāti cikitsitam

SYNONYMS

āmayaḥ—diseases; yaḥ ca—whatever; bhūtānām—of the living being; jāyate—become possible; yena—by the agency; suvrata—O good soul; tat—that; eva—very; hi—certainly; āmayam—disease; dravyam—thing; na—does it not; punāti—cure; cikitsitam—treated with.

TRANSLATION

O good soul, does not a thing, applied therapeutically, cure a disease which was caused by that very same thing?

<u>Proof through the Law of duality:</u>

V = No of Pathogen "V" which attack the body

1 x V = 1 x V

1 x V - 1 x V = 0

V != 0 -V != 0

V x 1/V = 1

Ot+1/Ot = 1/1 = Object at time t + 1 / Object at time t

V x 1/V – V x 1/V = 0

V – V = 0

Ev = Effect of pathogen "V"

Cv = Cause of effect of pathogen "V"

Ev – Ev = Cv - Cv

1/Ev = Anti-Effect of pathogen "V"

ACv = Cause of Anti-effect of pathogen "V"

1/Ev – 1/Ev = ACv – ACv

   Ev~0 => Cv = 0

Ev~ 0 => 1/ Ev ~ inf => ACv ~ inf

<u>Example:</u>

Consider agent A, which causes deformities in the body, with its effect quantified as E. For instance, let E = E' = 100 deformities per agent A. Applying the law of duality:

If,

$A(t+1) / A(t) = [E] / [E] = 1$

Then we also observe that

$A(t+1) / A(t) = [1/E] / [1/E] = 1$

This shows that when E occurs, 1/E must also occur. If E > 1/E, then E dominates, while if, E < 1/E, 1/E prevails.

In the case of a therapeutic (non-lethal) dose or preparation, where E approaches 0, we find that as E approaches zero, 1/E becomes very large. When E<<1/E, 1/E dominates, causing agent A to act as either a cure or a resistance molecule. For example, if E ≈ 0.00001 (or 10^{-6} deformities per agent A), then:

$1/E = 10^6$ agents A per deformity.

This means that a dose containing agent A can effectively counteract the disease, requiring 10^6 agents to cause a single deformity, thus acting as a resistance dose to fight off the disease.

The disease causing agent in low concentration:

$e = [Cc / Cs]$

An agent in low volumes will act to cure the disease instead of accelerating it.

As,

$e = Cc/Cs$

e proportional to 'V'

$e \sim 0$ as $V \sim 0$

$1/e \sim N$ as $1/V \sim N, N \gg 0$

A ready source of pathogens in low concentration is our urine and sweat, medicine systems exist which use these to cure oneself

The power of poisons:

$e = [Cc / Cs]$

A poison is something which accelerates or increases "e" such an element in low volumes will act to cure the disease instead of accelerating it.

As,

$e = Cc/Cs$

e proportional to 'V'

$e \sim 0$ as $V \sim 0$

$1/e \sim N$ as $1/V \sim N, N \gg 0$

Homeopathy

Homeopathy uses small doses of poisons which cause the very same diseases or condition to cure diseases. The proof for its efficacy is as follows: let the quantity of poison be Q ml

Q ml –has- N agents

N agents cause 1 deformities

Q' ml : Q × 10^-3 ml has : N × 10^-3 agents : 1 × 10^-3 deformities

Q' : E = 10^-3 deformities : 1/E = 10^3 deformities^-1

1/E >> E

So Q' becomes curative from lethal and cures the deformity, from the law of causation:

E = C1 × C2 × .. × Cn = Ce

1 / E = 1 / Ce

1/E >> E => 1/Ce >> Ce

1/Ce is the opposite of Ce and hence cures the deformity with it is dominating or being more than Ce.

Pharmacologically inert entities "A":

Pharmacologically inert substances with $E \approx 0$ possess the characteristic that $1/E \gg E$. This means that agent A, though inert, has a curative effect and can heal deformities, as explained by the law of causation.

We have:

E=C1×C2×...×Cn=Ce]

and

1/E=1/Ce

Since 1C >> Ce, we find that 1/Ce is much greater than Ce. This suggests that 1/Ce is the inverse of Ce, and thus, it counteracts or overpowers Ce, leading to the healing of the deformity when in contact with it.

Painkillers for pains:

An agent A causes a pain P, if agent A is in small quantity or in a deactivated state:

It causes pain P ~ 0 => 1/P ~ inf

What this suggests is what causes pain P in a limted quantity CL or in a deactivated state can alleviate that very pain.

Reference:

[1] ŚB 1.5.33 (vedabase.io) https://vedabase.io/en/library/sb/1/5/33/

Applications to Medical science : Mathematical model of The Immune System response

The human immune system is a complex network of cells, tissues, and organs that work together to defend the body against harmful pathogens like bacteria, viruses, and fungi.

It consists of two main components: the innate immune system, which provides immediate defense, and the adaptive immune system, which offers long-term protection through memory cells. The innate system includes physical barriers like skin, as well as cells like macrophages and neutrophils that attack invaders.

The adaptive immune system includes T cells and B cells, which recognize and remember specific pathogens. Antibodies produced by B cells neutralize pathogens. Lymph nodes, spleen, and bone marrow play crucial roles in immune function.

White blood cells are the primary soldiers in the immune response, with various types including lymphocytes and granulocytes. The immune system also regulates inflammation and wound healing. A healthy immune system requires balanced functioning, as overactive responses can lead to autoimmune diseases, while underactive responses result in increased vulnerability to infections. Vaccination helps the immune system recognize and fight pathogens before they cause illness.

Mathematical modelling of the immune system response using the "law of cause and effect"

The immune system, attacks harmful pathogens like bacteria, viruses, and fungi,

Lets understand how the immune system fights off harmful pathogens,

Let pathogen V be introduced into the body,

It induces an immune system response "Eiv", using the law of cause-effect,

$$Eiv = k2 \times Cn / Cd = k2 \times C1 \times C2 \times C3$$

Let the pathogen V introduced into the body have an efficacy : Ev

Ev is the negative effect on the body like deformities, fever etc.

Let the immune system response be production of cells (V') which fight of the pathogen V

$$Ev = k1 \, V$$

$$Eiv = V' = k2 \times Cn / Cd = k2' \times C1 \times C2 \times C3$$

if pathogen "V" stopped by V':

$$V \times V' = 1$$

Effect of V':

$$Ev' = k3 \, V'$$

$$Ev \times Ev' = 1$$

$$k3 \, V' \times k1 \, V = 1$$

$$V' = [\, 1/V \,] \times [\, 1 / [k3 \; k1] \,]$$

Effect of introducing weakened pathogens V" on the immune system response:

The immune system response is given by:

$$V' = [\, 1/V \,] \times [\, 1 / [k3 \; k1] \,]$$

Let's now look at the scenario of introducing weakened pathogens and pathogens in low concentration:

$$1 \times V = 1 \times V$$

$$1 \times V - 1 \times V = 0$$

$$V \times 1/V = 1$$

$Ot+1/Ot = 1/1$

$V \times 1/V - V \times 1/V = 0$

$V - V = 0$

$Ev - Ev = Cv - Cv$

$1/Ev - 1/Ev = Cv' - Cv'$

$Ev \sim 0 => Cv = 0$

$Ev \sim 0 => 1/ Ev \sim inf => Cv' \sim inf$

The anti-cause (Cv') is of a very large value when $Cv \to 0$ or the pathogen has been deactivated $Ev = 0$

Effect of a deactivated pathogen on immune system response:

Immune system repsonse is given by:

$V' = [1/V] \times [1 / [k3\, k1]$

$Ev = k1\, V$

$Ev \sim 0 => 1/ Ev \sim inf$

$V \sim 0 => V' \sim inf$

$V' = [1/V] \times [1 / [k3\, k1] = 1 / [Ev \times k3] = inf$

$V' \sim inf$ or a very large value

$V' = N \times [1/V]$

So the immune system response is amplified many-many times, this is how vaccination works and how we develop an immune system reponse to a pathogen when vaccinated or exposed to a deactivated pathogen

Effect of a low concentration of pathogen on immune system response:

$Ev = k1\, V$

Net effect $E'' = n\, Ev = k1\, [n\, V]$

Net immune system response $= E''iv = m1V' = k2 \times m1 \times [Cn / Cd] = k2' \times m1 \times [C1 \times C2 \times C3]$

if $E'' \sim 0$ as n is low

$E'' \times E''iv = 1$

$E'' => 0$ $E''iv = inf$ or a very large value $= m1V'$

    Assuming $E'' >> 0$ i.e. n is high

Net immune system response $= E''iv = m2V' = k2 \times m2 \times [Cn / Cd] = k2' \times m2 \times [C1 \times C2 \times C3]$

$E'' \times E''iv = 1$

$E'' >> 0$ $E''iv << 0$ or a very small value $= m2V'$

m1V' >> m2V'

So, the immune system gets a higher ability to fight the pathogen V compared to when a very large dose of pathogen V is injected in the body, an approach common to homeopathy

CHAPTER TWENTY-TWO

The Unification of the 4 forces: The Grand Unification Theory

Unification of gravity and other forces:
By the law of cause and effect:
E1 / E1 = C1 / C1 x C2 / C2 x C3 / C3 .... Cn/Cn
E1 = k Cn1 / Cn2

Statement 1: "0" produces the gravitational force, electrostatic force, electromagnetic force and strong and weak force holding entities in place or leads to their integration and prevents drift

Proof:
d = distance between entity1 and entity2
1/d = closeness between entity1 and entity2

From the law of cause and effect
d = Cn1 / Cn2
Cn1 = net cause
Cn2 = net anti-cause
if Cn1 = 0
d = 0
displacement s = s' by Force F
F.s' : Force F over distance s'
E = F x s' x cos[theta] = C1 x C2 x C3

Law of attraction

d = c1 c2 c3

c1 = 0 : d = 0 : <1/d = Inf> <presence of 0>

c1 = inf : d = inf : <1/d = 0> <absence of 0>

0 is the cause of 1/d between two entities

F x s = 0 if 1/d = 0 and

F x s = inf if 1/d = inf

F x s = E = k / d

F = -dE / dr

Cause-Effect data:

without which(effect) it cannot be

1/Cn1 = 0 | Cn1 = inf | 1/d = 0

1/Cn1 = 0 | Cn1 = inf | E = 0

"Absence is absent"

   with which(effect) | it is

1/Cn1 = inf | Cn1 = 0 | 1/d = inf

1/Cn1 = inf | Cn1 = 0 | E = inf

"Absence is infinite"

Equivalent to "0" being the cause of d and 1/E

or

1/d being the cause of E

   E1 = k1" / d

This is the potential due to one r = 0 pair, one in entity1 and another in entity2

E1 = Energy per pair

ET = Energy total = Total number of "0" pairs x E1

Total "0" pairs = K x e1 x e2

ET = Total "Energy" = K x e1 x e2 x k1" / d = K" e1 e2 /r

Force:

Fe = -dE/dr = - K" e1 e2 /r^2

   Or an entity e1 gets attracted to another entity e2 where both the entities exert a force of Fe on one another "integrating" into a single entity due to the attractive force of "0" on it.

Case1: Gravitational force:

The two entities are m1 and m2 and [r=0] in them are exerting force Fm:

Using the above generalization:

Ke' = G

e1 = m1

e2 = m2

r = r

Fm = G m1 m2 / [r^2]

Hence "0" is the cause of the gravitational force

Case2: Electrostatic force:

The two entities are q1 and q2 and [r=0] in them are exerting force Fq:

Using the above generalization:

Ke' = K

e1 = q1

e2 = q2

r = r

Fe = Ke' q1 q2 / [r^2]

Hence "0" is the cause of the electrostatic force

Case3: Electromagnetic force:

The charged particle in a magnetic field,

v = w/r

if charged particle in magnetic field "B"

and v = 0 it can be held at that place

if v != 0 it can be held at r = w/v

r - r1 = 0

It has to be held by a centipetral force

F = k c1 c2 x ... x cn

causes are q, B and for a centipetral force v x sin x [theta]

F = q B v sin[theta]

v is the speed of the particle (magnitude of the velocity),

B is the magnitude of the magnetic field,

theta is the angle between the velocity and the magnetic field vectors.

qvB=mv^2/r

r1=[mv]/[qB]

Here, r is the radius of curvature of the path of a charged particle with mass m and charge q, moving at a speed v that is perpendicular to a magnetic field of strength B.

r - r1 = 0

"0" holds or is the cause of the sustaining force, sustaining here the charged particle in a circular motion of radius "r1"

Hence "0" is the cause of the electromagnetic force

The Yukawa potential for "strong force" and "weak force":

We consider properties of the Yukawa potential,

V (r) = [k/r] x e ^ [−r/alpha] = [k/r] x [1 / e ^ [r/alpha]]

?: The mass of the particle

?: The radial distance to the particle

?: A scaling constant that determines the range of the potential

"α" represents a constant related to the range of the force

Cn1 = 0 => r = 0 => 1/r = inf => F . s' => V ~ inf

Cn1 = inf => r = inf => 1/r = 0 => F . s' => F x s' x cos[theta] ~ F x s' => V~0

"0" or "1/r" and "e1" and "e2" are the cause of the yukawa potential

e1 and e2 are the entities between which the Yukawa potential holds

r is the distance between them

"0" is contained in e1 and e2

Conclusion:

The four forces are ultimately the force of attraction by 0's in like entities hence they are the same underlying force in essence.

CHAPTER TWENTY-THREE

The Theory of Everything

In this chapter, we in a set of equations explain the working of the entire Universe and capture its physics

The "Theory of Everything" summarized is:
1. Whatever exists falls into the categories of
1. Substance/Genus (qg)
2. Attribute (qd)
3. Action (A)
2. Cause is defined without which effect cannot be,
Causes are of two types:
1. Instrumental cause
2. Material cause

1. Law of action and reaction:
E – E = 0
E = Action
-E = Reaction
Action and Reaction are equal and opposite

2. Law of action and consequence:
$E_{t12} - E_{t34} = 0$

E_{t12} = Action performed at time t12
E_{t34} = Action experienced at time t34
What is committed is experienced

3. Law of cause and effect:
E/E = [C1/C1] x ... x [Cn/Cn]

E = Effect
C1 = cause_1
Cn = cause_n

E - E = [C1 x C2 x .. x Cn] - [C1 x C2 x .. x Cn] = Ot+1@x - Ot@x = {0}
E = qg, qd, A, Obj
    qg = C1 x ... x Cn / C2 x ... x C2n = C1n / C2n
qd = C3 x ... x Cn / C4 x ... x C4n = C3n / C4n

A = Modification and Movement
R = Rate of modification and movement
E(R) and 1/E(1/R) occur which have net cause Ca1 and Cr2
Using the Law of cause and effect:
Rw = Ca1 / Cr2
Rw+ = + Ca1 / Cr2 or Rw- = - Ca1 / Cr2
Ca causes action
Cr resists change here action
    The things that change are : form f, quality q, position x
using the equation: y = mx + c
f2 = Rw x tw + f0 -[1]
q2 = Rw x tw + q0 -[2]
x2 = Rw x tw + x0 -[3]
If Rw is a function use definitc integrals to calculate the value

<u>Another action is illumination:</u>
I = illumination
According to the law of cause and effect
E(I) and 1/E(1/I) occur which have net cause Ci1 and Cr2
Ci causes illumination
Cr resists change here illumination

I1 = Ci1 / Cr1 -[4]

<u>The controller of Ca, Ci, Cr:</u>
The controller of Ca, Ci and Cr causes them to:
1. Move
2. Pair
3. Act

Movement:

$Ot+1\_x1 - Ot\_x1 = 2Ca1 - 2Ca1 = 0$

$Ot+1\_x1 - Ot\_x1 + Ot+1\_x2 - Ot\_x2 = \{Ca1 - Ca1\} + \{Ca1 - Ca1\}$

Pair:

$Ot+1\_x1 - Ot\_x1 = \{Ca1+Ca2\} - \{Ca1+Ca2\} = \{Ca1/Ca2\} - \{Ca1/Ca2\} = 0$

Act:

$Ot+1\_x1 - Ot\_x1 = \{Ca1+Ca2\} - \{Ca1+Ca2\} = \{Ca1/Ca2\} - \{Ca1/Ca2\} = \{E1\} - \{E1\} = 0$

"0" causes them to move, pair and act hence it is the cause of all actions, "0" is the controller of all actions

The cosmic form and its controller:

1. { 0 x Inf } or "Infinito" creates, sustains, and transforms the universe.

2. { 0 x Inf } is the Universe which through "0" {Ca, Ci, Cf} creates, sustain and transforms it

$\{0xInf\} = Ut+1 - Ut = \{ Ot+1\_x1 - Ot\_x1 \} + \{ Ot+1\_x2 - Ot\_x2 \} + \{ Ot+1\_x3 - Ot\_x3 \}$

Transformation:

$\{0xInf\} = Ut+1 - Ut = \{ Ot+1\_x1 - Ot\_x1 + \{c1-c1\} + \{c2-c2\} + \{c3-c3\}\} + \{ Ot+1\_x2 - Ot\_x2 \} + \{ Ot+1\_x3 - Ot\_x3 \}$

$\{0xInf\} = Ut+1 - Ut = \{ \{c1c2c3-c1c2c3\} \} + \{ Ot+1\_x2 - Ot\_x2 \} + \{ Ot+1\_x3 - Ot\_x3 \}$

$\{0xInf\} = Ut+1 - Ut = \{ O"t+1\_x1 - O"t\_x1 \} + \{ Ot+1\_x2 - Ot\_x2 \} + \{ Ot+1\_x3 - Ot\_x3 \}$

Creation:

$\{0xInf\} = Ut+1 - Ut = \{ Ot+1\_x1 - Ot\_x1 \} + \{ Ot+1\_x2 - Ot\_x2 \} + \{ Ot+1\_x3 - Ot\_x3 \}$

$\{0xInf\} = Ut+1 - Ut = \{\{c1-c1\} + \{c2-c2\} + \{c3-c3\}\} + \{ Ot+1\_x1 - Ot\_x1 \} + \{ Ot+1\_x2 - Ot\_x2 \} + \{ Ot+1\_x3 - Ot\_x3 \}$

$\{0xInf\} = Ut+1 - Ut = \{ c1c2c3-c1c2c3 \} + \{ Ot+1\_x1 - Ot\_x1 \} + \{ Ot+1\_x2 - Ot\_x2 \} + \{ Ot+1\_x3 - Ot\_x3 \}$

$\{0xInf\} = Ut+1 - Ut = \{ Oc\_t+1\_xn - Oc\_t\_xn \} + \{ Ot+1\_x1 - Ot\_x1 \} + \{ Ot+1\_x2 - Ot\_x2 \} + \{ Ot+1\_x3 - Ot\_x3 \}$

<u>Sustaining:</u>

$\{0xInf\}$ = Ut+1 - Ut = { Ot+1_x1 - Ot_x1 + {c1-c1} + {c2-c2} + {c3-c3}} + { Ot+1_x2 - Ot_x2 } + { Ot+1_x3 - Ot_x3 }

$\{0xInf\}$ = Ut+1 - Ut = { {c1c2c3-c1c2c3} } + { Ot+1_x2 - Ot_x2 } + { Ot+1_x3 - Ot_x3 }

$\{0xInf\}$ = Ut+1 - Ut = { Ot+1_x1 - Ot_x1 } + { Ot+1_x2 - Ot_x2 } + { Ot+1_x3 - Ot_x3 }

CHAPTER TWENTY-FOUR

The Universe in an Equation

The Multiverse-Universe in an equation:

e1{ e2 + {O1_t+1{e3} - O1t{e3}} + {O2_t+1{e3} - O2_t{e3}} + ... } x { e2' + {O1'_t+1{e3} - O1'_t{e3}} + {O2'_t+1{e3} - O2'_t{e3}} + ... } x .... = 1

The Above is the multiverse equation:

1st Universe = { e2 + {O1_t+1{e3} - O1_t{e3}} + {O2_t+1{e3} - O2_t{e3}} + ... }

2nd Universe = { e2' + {O1'_t+1{e3} - O1'_t{e3}} + {O2'_t+1{e3} - O2'_t{e3}} + ... }

e1 = 1

e2, e2', e2" = 1

e3 = 1

It can written in another way:

1{{O1_t+1{e3}/O1_t{e3}} x {O2_t+1{e3}/O2_t{e3}} + ... } x {O1'_t+1{e3}/O1'_t{e3}} x {O2'_t+1{e3}/O2'_t{e3}} + ... } x .... = 1

The Above is the multiverse equation:

1st Universe = e2 = 1 = {{O1_t+1{e3} / O1_t{e3}} x {O2_t+1{e3} / O2_t{e3}} + ... }

2nd Universe = e2' = 1 = {{O1'_t+1{e3} / O1'_t{e3}} x {O2'_t+1{e3} / O2'_t{e3}} + ... }

e1 = 1

e2, e2', e2" = 1

e3 = 1

All are manifestations of Existence:

1. e1

2. e2

3. e3

e1{ e2 + {O1_t+1{e3} - O1t{e3}} + {O2_t+1{e3} - O2_t{e3}} + ... } = 1
O1_t+1{e3} - O1t{e3} = 0
The basic relations between an object or an entity in any universe and 1 or existence is found using the law of cause and effect:

E1/E1 = [C1/C1] x [C2/C2] x [C3/C3] x .... x [Cn/Cn]

1. <u>Protected-protector:</u>

C1/C1 = E/E

Counteracting factors absent when something is sustained

1 = [Ot+1/Ot] x $\prod$ { [1/cac_n / 1/cac_n] [cac_n / cac_n] }

cac_n = counter-acting cause n

Cause is "1" or Existence

2. <u>Sustiner and sustained</u>

e3 sustains Ot or "Existence" sustains Ot if it was "0" it wouldnt sustain e3

C2/C2 = E/E

1 = [Ot+1/Ot] x $\prod$ [ne_n/ne_n]

ne_n = Neccesity n

Cause is "1" or Existence

3. <u>Controller-controlled</u>

On_t+1{e3} - On_t{e3} = 0

On'_t+1{e3} - On'_t{e3} = 0

0 controls On "Object n" it can induce a change in the object or move i.e. it controlls its qualities, time and position

4. <u>Master-servitor</u>

e1{ e2 + {O1_t+1{e3} - O1t{e3}} + {O2_t+1{e3} - O2_t{e3}} + ... } = 1

[1][1]{ 1 + {O1_t+1{[1]} - O1t{[1]}} + {O2_t+1{[1]} - O2_t{[1]}} + ... } = 1

{ O1_t+1{[1]} - O1t{[1]} } provides a [1] to e1 which is common to the bracket

hence { O1_t+1{[1]} - O1t{[1]} } sustains e1 or serves its purpose

So if { O1_t+1{[1]} - O1t{[1]} } exists it sustains e1 and serves its purpose, if it doesnt serve the purpose it falls of the Universe and ceases to exist.

Another proof:

E/E = C/C

$1\{1\} = Ot+1/Ot$

$[Bt+1/Bt] \times \{1\} = Ot+1/Ot$

Ot is sustained to sustain "Existence" or entity "Bt" which sustains "Existence" indirectly

$1\{1\}$ can be interpreted as:

1. Sustaining an entity N or the "Universe itself"

2. Giving "Existence" bliss

5. Owned-Owner

$A = 1 \times A$

1 is the owner

A is the owned

5.1 Contined-Container

$O1 = 1 \times O1/1$

1 is the container

O1 is the contained

5.2 Pervaded-Pervader

$A = 1 \times A$

1 is the pervader

A is the pervaded

CHAPTER TWENTY-FIVE

Summary

<u>Law of action and reaction:</u>

E – E = 0

E = Action

-E = Reaction

    Action and Reaction are equal and opposite

<u>Law of action and consequence:</u>

$E\_t12 - E\_t34 = 0$

E_t12 = Action performed at time t12

E_t34 = Action experienced at time t34

    What is committed is experienced

<u>Law of cause and effect:</u>

    E/E = [C1/C1] x ... x [C2/C2]

    E = Effect

C1 = cause1

C2 = cause2

<u>Law of duality:</u>

    E x 1/E = 1

E = entity E

1/E = opposite of entity E occur together

    <u>Action/Change Equation:</u>

    [x + { [p1/ap1] x [tw1] – [p2/ap2] x [tw2] }] – {xw} = {0}

p1/ap1 > p2/ap2 Increase

p1/ap1 < p2/ap2 Decrease

p1/ap1 = p2/ap2 Being

p1/ap1 < p2/ap2 till 0 | Removal

pn = "acto" quality (controlled)

apn = "resisto" quality (controlled)

x = quality (controlled)

tw1 = controlled time

tw2 = controlled time

{0} = controller

{xw} = value willed by controller "0"

Illumination Equation:

vl / vl = [L1 / L1] x ... x [ap1 / ap1]

L1 = "Lumo" quality

ap1 = "resisto" quality

   { [L1/ap1] x [tw1] } – {Iw} = {0}

   {0} = controller

{Iw} = value willed by controller "0"

The cosmic form:

O1 = O1x1 = q1A1

O2 = O2x1 = q2A2

On = Onx1 = qnAn

Ut2/Ut1 = O1/O1 x O2/O2 x ... x On/On

Ut2 = [O1 x 1] x [O2 x 1] x ... x [On x 1]

1 x 1 x 1 x .. x 1 = 1

Ut2 = [O1] x [O2] x ... x [On] x [1]

Ut2 = [q1A1] x [q2A2] x ... x [qnAn] x [1]

   1 has all qualities

1 performs all actions

all are the qualities, actions and parts of "1"

O1 can be your sister and O2 can be your friend's sister,

but they are one as it is only 1 acting through them

something which can be stated as "All Indians are my brothers and sisters"

<u>The medicine law:</u>
if an entity "B" causes disease, the same entity in a "non lethal form" or "dose" cures the disease

C ~ 0 | 1/C ~ Inf

C = disease causing ability

1/C = disease resisting or curing ability

<u>The trade-economy equation:</u>

$$\{P - \{Pw\}\} + [L][1]\{ O' - O' \} = 0$$

P = person

Pw = Selected person

O' = {O1, O2, O3, O4 ....} for L = 1

O' = {O1', O2', O3', O4' ....} for L = 0.5

O' = Exchanged object or value of exchanged object depends on the value of L

L = 1 means Object O' exchanged with 1

L = 1 means Object O' exchanged with 0.5 "1"

<u>Law of cause and effect:</u>

$$E/E = [C1/C1] \, x \ldots x \, [Cn/Cn]$$

E = Effect

C1 = cause_1

Cn = cause_n

$$E - E = [C1 \, x \, C2 \, x \, .. \, x \, Cn] - [C1 \, x \, C2 \, x \, .. \, x \, Cn] = Ot+1@x - Ot@x = \{0\}$$

E = qg, qd, A, Obj

{0} is the controller or the cause of the cause and hence effect at a particular location x and time t

Obj = [qg qd A]

qg = C1 x ... x Cn / C2 x ... x C2n = C1n / C2n

qd = C3 x ... x Cn / C4 x ... x C4n = C3n / C4n

A = Modification and Movement

Del q = k x [C3 / C4] x t

Del xm = k x [C3 / C4] x t